ORPHAN GIRL

The Other Voice in Early Modern Europe:
The Toronto Series, 45

MEDIEVAL AND RENAISSANCE
TEXTS AND STUDIES

VOLUME 492

The Other Voice in
Early Modern Europe:
The Toronto Series

SERIES EDITORS Margaret L. King *and* Albert Rabil, Jr.
SERIES EDITOR, ENGLISH TEXTS Elizabeth H. Hageman

Previous Publications in the Series

MADRE MARÍA ROSA
Journey of Five Capuchin Nuns
Edited and translated by Sarah E. Owens
Volume 1, 2009

GIOVAN BATTISTA ANDREINI
Love in the Mirror: A Bilingual Edition
Edited and translated by Jon R. Snyder
Volume 2, 2009

RAYMOND DE SABANAC AND SIMONE ZANACCHI
Two Women of the Great Schism: The Revelations *of Constance de Rabastens by Raymond de Sabanac and* Life of the Blessed Ursulina of Parma *by Simone Zanacchi*
Edited and translated by Renate Blumenfeld-Kosinski and Bruce L. Venarde
Volume 3, 2010

OLIVA SABUCO DE NANTES BARRERA
The True Medicine
Edited and translated by Gianna Pomata
Volume 4, 2010

LOUISE-GENEVIÈVE GILLOT DE SAINCTONGE
Dramatizing Dido, Circe, and Griselda
Edited and translated by Janet Levarie Smarr
Volume 5, 2010

PERNETTE DU GUILLET
Complete Poems: A Bilingual Edition
Edited by Karen Simroth James
Translated by Marta Rijn Finch
Volume 6, 2010

ANTONIA PULCI
Saints' Lives and Bible Stories for the Stage: A Bilingual Edition
Edited by Elissa B. Weaver
Translated by James Wyatt Cook
Volume 7, 2010

VALERIA MIANI
Celinda, A Tragedy: A Bilingual Edition
Edited by Valeria Finucci
Translated by Julia Kisacky
Annotated by Valeria Finucci and Julia Kisacky
Volume 8, 2010

Enchanted Eloquence: Fairy Tales by Seventeenth-Century French Women Writers
Edited and translated by Lewis C. Seifert and Domna C. Stanton
Volume 9, 2010

GOTTFRIED WILHELM LEIBNIZ, SOPHIE, ELECTRESS OF HANOVER AND QUEEN SOPHIE CHARLOTTE OF PRUSSIA
Leibniz and the Two Sophies: The Philosophical Correspondence
Edited and translated by Lloyd Strickland
Volume 10, 2011

In Dialogue with the Other Voice in Sixteenth-Century Italy: Literary and Social Contexts for Women's Writing
Edited by Julie D. Campbell and Maria Galli Stampino
Volume 11, 2011

The Other Voice in
Early Modern Europe:
The Toronto Series

Previous Publications in the Series

SISTER GIUSTINA NICCOLINI
The Chronicle of Le Murate
Edited and translated by Saundra Weddle
Volume 12, 2011

LIUBOV KRICHEVSKAYA
No Good without Reward: Selected Writings: A Bilingual Edition
Edited and translated by Brian James Baer
Volume 13, 2011

ELIZABETH COOKE HOBY RUSSELL
The Writings of an English Sappho
Edited by Patricia Phillippy
With translations by Jaime Goodrich
Volume 14, 2011

LUCREZIA MARINELLA
Exhortations to Women and to Others If They Please
Edited and translated by Laura Benedetti
Volume 15, 2012

MARGHERITA DATINI
Letters to Francesco Datini
Translated by Carolyn James and Antonio Pagliaro
Volume 16, 2012

DELARIVIER MANLEY AND MARY PIX
English Women Staging Islam, 1696–1707
Edited and introduced by Bernadette Andrea
Volume 17, 2012

CECILIA DEL NACIMIENTO
Journeys of a Mystic Soul in Poetry and Prose
Introduction and prose translations by Kevin Donnelly
Poetry translations by Sandra Sider
Volume 18, 2012

LADY MARGARET DOUGLAS AND OTHERS
The Devonshire Manuscript: A Women's Book of Courtly Poetry
Edited and introduced by Elizabeth Heale
Volume 19, 2012

ARCANGELA TARABOTTI
Letters Familiar and Formal
Edited and translated by Meredith K. Ray and Lynn Lara Westwater
Volume 20, 2012

PERE TORRELLAS AND JUAN DE FLORES
Three Spanish Querelle *Texts:* Grisel and Mirabella, The Slander against Women, *and* The Defense of Ladies against Slanderers: *A Bilingual Edition and Study*
Edited and translated by Emily C. Francomano
Volume 21, 2013

BARBARA TORELLI BENEDETTI
Partenia, a Pastoral Play: A Bilingual Edition
Edited and translated by Lisa Sampson and Barbara Burgess-Van Aken
Volume 22, 2013

The Other Voice in
Early Modern Europe:
The Toronto Series

Previous Publications in the Series

François Rousset, Jean Liebault, Jacques Guillemeau, Jacques Duval and Louis De Serres
Pregnancy and Birth in Early Modern France: Treatises by Caring Physicians and Surgeons (1581–1625)
Edited and translated by Valerie Worth-Stylianou
Volume 23, 2013

Mary Astell
The Christian Religion, as Professed by a Daughter of the Church of England
Edited by Jacqueline Broad
Volume 24, 2013

Sophia of Hanover
Memoirs (1630–1680)
Edited and translated by Sean Ward
Volume 25, 2013

Katherine Austen
Book M: A London Widow's Life Writings
Edited by Pamela S. Hammons
Volume 26, 2013

Anne Killigrew
"My Rare Wit Killing Sin": Poems of a Restoration Courtier
Edited by Margaret J. M. Ezell
Volume 27, 2013

Tullia d'Aragona and Others
The Poems and Letters of Tullia d'Aragona and Others: A Bilingual Edition
Edited and translated by Julia L. Hairston
Volume 28, 2014

Luisa de Carvajal y Mendoza
The Life and Writings of Luisa de Carvajal y Mendoza
Edited and translated by Anne J. Cruz
Volume 29, 2014

Russian Women Poets of the Eighteenth and Early Nineteenth Centuries: A Bilingual Edition
Edited and translated by Amanda Ewington
Volume 30, 2014

Jacques du Bosc
L'Honnête Femme: The Respectable Woman in Society *and the* New Collection of Letters and Responses by Contemporary Women
Edited and translated by Sharon Diane Nell and Aurora Wolfgang
Volume 31, 2014

Lady Hester Pulter
Poems, Emblems, and *The Unfortunate Florinda*
Edited by Alice Eardley
Volume 32, 2014

Jeanne Flore
Tales and Trials of Love, Concerning Venus's Punishment of Those Who Scorn True Love and Denounce Cupid's Sovereignity: A Bilingual Edition and Study
Edited and translated by Kelly Digby Peebles
Poems translated by Marta Rijn Finch
Volume 33, 2014

The Other Voice in
Early Modern Europe:
The Toronto Series

SERIES EDITORS Margaret L. King *and* Albert Rabil, Jr.
SERIES EDITOR, ENGLISH TEXTS Elizabeth H. Hageman

Previous Publications in the Series

VERONICA GAMBARA
Complete Poems: A Bilingual Edition
Critical introduction by Molly M. Martin
Edited and translated by Molly M. Martin and Paola Ugolini
Volume 34, 2014

CATHERINE DE MÉDICIS AND OTHERS
Portraits of the Queen Mother: Polemics, Panegyrics, Letters
Translation and study by Leah L. Chang and Katherine Kong
Volume 35, 2014

FRANÇOISE PASCAL, MARIE-CATHERINE DESJARDINS, ANTOINETTE DESHOULIÈRES, AND CATHERINE DURAND
Challenges to Traditional Authority: Plays by French Women Authors, 1650–1700
Edited and translated by Perry Gethner
Volume 36, 2015

FRANCISZKA URSZULA RADZIWIŁŁOWA
Selected Drama and Verse
Edited by Patrick John Corness and Barbara Judkowiak
Translated by Patrick John Corness
Translation Editor Aldona Zwierzyńska-Coldicott
Introduction by Barbara Judkowiak
Volume 37, 2015

DIODATA MALVASIA
Writings on the Sisters of San Luca and Their Miraculous Madonna
Edited and translated by Danielle Callegari and Shannon McHugh
Volume 38, 2015

MARGARET VAN NOORT
Spiritual Writings of Sister Margaret of the Mother of God (1635–1643)
Edited by Cordula van Wyhe
Translated by Susan M. Smith
Volume 39, 2015

GIOVAN FRANCESCO STRAPAROLA
The Pleasant Nights
Edited and translated by Suzanne Magnanini
Volume 40, 2015

ANGÉLIQUE DE SAINT-JEAN ARNAULD D'ANDILLY
Writings of Resistance
Edited and translated by John J. Conley, S.J.
Volume 41, 2015

FRANCESCO BARBARO
The Wealth of Wives: A Fifteenth-Century Marriage Manual
Edited and translated by Margaret L. King
Volume 42, 2015

The Other Voice in
Early Modern Europe:
The Toronto Series

SERIES EDITORS Margaret L. King *and* Albert Rabil, Jr.
SERIES EDITOR, ENGLISH TEXTS Elizabeth H. Hageman

Previous Publications in the Series

JEANNE D'ALBRET
Letters from the Queen of Navarre with an Ample Declaration
Edited and translated by Kathleen M. Llewellyn, Emily E. Thompson, and Colette H. Winn
Volume 43, 2016

BATHSUA MAKIN AND MARY MORE WITH A REPLY TO MORE BY ROBERT WHITEHALL
Educating English Daughters: Late Seventeenth-Century Debates
Edited by Frances Teague and Margaret J. M. Ezell
Associate Editor Jessica Walker
Volume 44, 2016

ANNA STANISŁAWSKA

Orphan Girl

A Transaction, or an Account of the Entire Life of an Orphan Girl by way of Plaintful Threnodies in the Year 1685

The Aesop Episode

~

Verse translation, introduction, and commentary by

BARRY KEANE

Iter Academic Press
Toronto, Ontario

Arizona Center for Medieval and Renaissance Studies
Tempe, Arizona

2016

Iter Academic Press
Tel: 416/978-7074 Email: iter@utoronto.ca
Fax: 416/978-1668 Web: www.itergateway.org

Arizona Center for Medieval and Renaissance Studies
Tel: 480/965-5900 Email: mrts@acmrs.org
Fax: 480/965-1681 Web: acmrs.org

Printed in Canada.

Library of Congress Cataloging-in-Publication Data

Names: Stanisławska, Anna, approximately 1651–1700 or 1701, author. | Keane, Barry, 1972– translator writer of added commentary.

Title: Orphan girl : a transaction, or an account of the entire life of an orphan girl by way of plaintful threnodies in the year 1685 : the Aesop episode / verse translation, introduction, and commentary by Barry Keane.

Description: Toronto, Ontario : Iter Academic Press ; Tempe, Arizona : Arizona Center for Medieval and Renaissance Studies, 2016. | Series: The Other Voice in Early Modern Europe. The Toronto Series ; 45 | Series: Medieval and Renaissance texts and studies ; volume 492 | Based on the author's autobiographical poem with title: Transakcyja: albo, Opisanie całego życia jednej sieroty, przez Żałosne treny od tejże samej pisane roku 1685; per the translator, the translation ends at the point where the author claims her freedom from Aesop [her husband] and is looking forward with some trepidation to her future. | Includes bibliographical references and index.

Identifiers: LCCN 2015043273 | ISBN 9780866985475 (pbk. : alk. paper)

Subjects: LCSH: Stanisławska, Anna, approximately 1651–1700 or 1701--Poetry. | Women poets, Polish--17th century--Biography--Poetry. | Wife abuse--Poetry. | Stanisławska, Anna, approximately 1651–1700 or 1701--Translations into English.

Classification: LCC PG7157.S73 T7313 2016 | DDC 891.8/514--dc23

LC record available at http://lccn.loc.gov/2015043273

Cover illustration:

MP 4310. Unknown Polish painter. Portrait of Anna of the Stanisławski Family. 1. Warszycka 2. Oleśnicka, 2. Zbąska; Canvas 87x 67. Copyright by Piotr Ligier/ The National Museum of Warsaw.

Cover design:

Maureen Morin, Information Technology Services, University of Toronto Libraries.

Typesetting and production:

Iter Academic Press.

Contents

Foreword

"The days of my bondage begin," Anna Stanisławska observes as, the marriage rite completed, the wedding guests sit down "and brace themselves for the speeches" (Threnody 6, Stanza 43). She tells the story of her coerced marriage and eventual triumphant liberation in twenty-nine verse "threnodies," or lamentations, modeled on the threnodies composed a century earlier by the Polish Renaissance humanist and poet Jan Kochanowski for the death of his young daughter. Her imitation was appropriate in that she, too, lamented the death of a daughter: herself, the daughter of a father who for selfish and mercenary motives conveyed her into the arms of an impossible husband, but who in the end, from the grave, through his surrogates, achieved the dissolution of that unjust contract.

It was central to the condition of women in all civilizations prior to our own modern and industrialized one that marriage choice was not a woman's to make. It was the business of families, often negotiated with women elders consulting, but ultimately concluded in the interests of clan heads and property-owners. Such was the situation in Renaissance and early modern Europe, when we first hear in literature—lyric verse, drama, romance, and novella—protests against this particular kind of coercion. But to my knowledge, there is no autobiographical account in any European language of the experience of coerced marriage so complete and powerful as that of Anna Stanisławska. The first-person epic account of her life is here translated from the Polish into English verse by Barry Keane, a noted Irish poet, translator of Polish poetry, and scholarly exponent of Polish literature. His limpid and compelling translation conveys the pain experienced by this orphan girl forced into marriage with a bumbling monster who aspired to kill her.

Margaret L. King
January 2016

Acknowledgments

Although never the easiest of undertakings, I feel tremendously privileged to have had the opportunity to work on such a unique and powerful poetic text. I greatly appreciate the support and encouragement I have received from my department colleagues, Aniela Korzeniowska and Agnieszka Piskorska, and this appreciation extends to Jerzy Jarniewicz, Ewa Ledóchowicz, David Malcolm, Piotr Urbański and Piotr Wilczek, all of whom have helped me in a myriad of ways. I would also like to mention the unwavering support and friendship I have received in Ireland from Michael Cronin, John Dillon, Justin Doherty, Michael Hinds, and Tom Galvin. I owe an inestimable debt to Margaret King, who has been tremendously inspiring, and so generous and patient in steering this project through to completion. And also for their great efforts and support, I would like to express my warmest thanks and appreciation to Margaret English-Haskin and Anabela Piersol.

On a personal note, I would like to express my sadness that I have been unable to show my completed work to the folklorist, Dáithí Ó hÓgáin, and my father, Barry snr., both of whom passed away in recent times. Great friends with one another, both men encouraged and inspired me to write poetry and they will always be the imagined readers whom I most want to impress. I must also express my gratitude to my mother Vera, my brother Declan, and sisters Orla, Lynn and Rona for a lifetime of golden memories. And finally, to my wife, Agata, and our little girls, Julia and Karolina, who are the great contentment and joy at the heart of everything I do, and to whom this book is dedicated.

Introduction

The Other Voice

Writing years after the terrible events that colored her life forever, Anna Stanisławska (1651–1701) meticulously reconstructed in an autobiographical epic poem the episode of her forced marriage to a deviant who terrorized and humiliated her at every turn. It is a poetic account that represents a remarkable tale of triumph in the face of overwhelming domestic oppression. The manner by which Stanisławska wrested back control over her life was an unprecedented feat for a woman in the time in which she lived, for not only did she escape the clutches of a feared magnate family but managed to secure a divorce and marry "for love" soon afterwards. The poem is an unparalleled and compelling work in terms of its exploration of a woman's situation in marriage and the stark choices posed by a coerced life in the seventeenth century. Long unknown to Polish letters, Anna Stanisławska may be rightfully hailed as one of the most important "other" and certainly "forgotten" voices of the Baroque era, grappling as she did with the dark truths and eternal hopes that underpinned so many women's lives.

Awaiting Discovery

In 1890, during the course of research in the archives of the Imperial Public Library of St. Petersburg, the Polish Slavic scholar, Aleksander Brückner, discovered the late seventeenth-century manuscript of a lengthy poem with the equally lengthy and rather shocking title: *Transakcyja albo opisanie życia jednej sieroty przez żałosne treny od tejże samej pisane roku 1685* [A Transaction, or an Account of the Life of an Orphan Girl by way of Plaintful Threnodies Written in the Year 1685]. The poem ran for 254 pages; contained 654 stanzas, was divided into 77 threnodies of differing length, and was bookended by opening and closing poems to the reader. The work also had brief margin notes on the left hand side of the pages (in this book, the margin notes are to be found on the right-hand side of the poem), which were placed beside certain stanzas. More curiously still, like a petition to the Holy Family to bless the endeavor, the top left-hand corner of the title page featured the names of Jesus, Mary and Joseph.

Three years after the discovery of the manuscript, in what was the first article devoted to the poem, Brückner revealed that the author was Anna Stanisławska, surnamed Warszycka by her first marriage, Oleśnicka by her second, and Zbąska by her third, and judged the work to be a vivid account of a momentous life lived in momentous times.[1] Some years later, however, the scholar would be less effusive. Describing the work as a life in verse intermingled with never-ending complaints about the workings of Fortune, Brückner asserted that the manuscript boasted "terrible poetry" [*wiersze marne*], but stated, in turn, that it was one of the most fascinating works to come out of seventeenth-century Poland.[2] His pronouncement perhaps unintentionally set the tone for the adverse judgments that followed. What is more, by referring to the poet throughout his article as Anna Stanisławska, Brückner also established a tradition whereby she would henceforth be referred to most often by her maiden name.

Decades of difficult negotiations with St. Petersburg, which after the Russian Revolution became Leningrad, meant that *Orphan Girl* (as the full title of Stanisławska's *Transaction* is abbreviated in this volume) would not be read by the *fin de siècle* generation of Young Poland, or indeed the generation of post-World War I writers. In 1934, the manuscript was brought from Leningrad to the National Library of Warsaw as part of a larger exchange of manuscripts, and this exchange coincided with the publication of the entire manuscript, as edited by Ida Kotowa, who had made recourse to facsimiles of the poem.[3] Kotowa also included in her introduction a letter dated May 5, 1699, from Stanisławska to Franciszek Bieniecki, which is preserved in the Museo Correr of Venice. Although the letter is mostly dictated, the poet did extend her salutations in her own handwriting, and so revealed beyond a shadow of a doubt that the Anna Stanisławska-Zbąska of both letter and poem were one and the same person.

A review of *Orphan Girl* by Renaissance scholar, Tadeusz Sinko, in the Kraków broadsheet *Czas* [Time][4] drew for the first time the attention of a wide number of potential readers to this literary pearl. However, the fact that Kotowa's edition had a small print-run, and that it was aimed principally at a narrow group of Polish literary scholars, meant that Stanisławska would remain a largely unknown figure in Poland. Having been relegated at the outset by Brückner to the status of third rate, the case was rarely made forcibly enough that *Orphan Girl* was deserving of a celebrated place in the Polish canon, which would inevitably have won for the poem the kind of readership that comes with being an anthologized work.

1. Aleksander Brückner, "Wiersze zbieranej drużyny: Pierwsza autorka polska i jej autobiografia wierszem," *Biblioteka Warszawska* 4 (1893), 424–29. Translations of Polish titles are given in the Bibliography.

2. Brückner *Dzieje literatury polskiej w zarysie*, vol. 1 (Warsaw: Gebethner i Wolff, 1908), 366.

3. The edition of Ida Kotowa, with her introduction and notes: *Transakcyja albo opisanie całego życia jednej sieroty przez żałosne treny od tejże samej pisane roku 1685* (Kraków: Polska Akademia Umiejętności, 1935). Kotowa discusses this manuscript exchange from Leningrad to Warsaw in the introduction, 18, for which see also Dariusz Rott, *Kobieta z przemalowanego portretu* (Katowice: Wydawnictwo Uniwersytetu Śląskiego, 2004), 32–33.

4. Tadeusz Sinko, "Trzy małżeństwa jednej sieroty," *Czas* 109 (1935): 5.

If prospects for the work's reception remained slight in the 1930s, World War II proved even more injurious to Stanisławska's legacy, as the precious manuscript was destroyed in the conflagration of the Warsaw Uprising. Happily, over the past two decades a growing number of academics have written of the power and value of *Orphan Girl* as a literary and historical work. That said, scholarship has its limitations when it comes to popularizing seventeenth-century poems, and Anna Stanisławska's unique contribution to the literary life of her homeland is still unknown to many.

The Historical Backdrop

As we shall see in this brief historical overview, Anna Stanisławska and her contemporaries lived in exceptionally challenging times.[5] The long reign of Swedish-born Zygmunt III Waza from 1587 to 1632 saw the Polish-Lithuanian Commonwealth obtain dizzy heights in terms of its military and political reach. However, overconfident of his position, Zygmunt made injudicious claims on the throne of Sweden and attempted disastrous conquests of Moscow and Moldavia. Zygmunt's legacy would hinge on his foreign policy in respect of Sweden and Russia. He had been crowned king of Sweden in 1594, but the regency council distrusted his Catholic bias, insisting that he recognize Lutheranism as Sweden's state religion. It was also demanded of Zygmunt that his uncle hold the reins of power in his absence. In 1598, in an ill-considered move designed to wrest back control of Sweden, the Polish king staged a naval invasion, which soon descended into farce. Captured and dethroned, Zygmunt had to barter for his own life by denouncing his own Swedish supporters, who were subsequently executed.[6] The two countries would also clash over Poland-Lithuania's claim to Livonia, which was held by Sweden. This led to a protracted war with Sweden, which, with minor intervals, lasted until 1629.

Zygmunt was mistrusted amongst the Polish gentry for both his marital alliance with the Hapsburg family and for his attempts at political reform designed to weaken the power of the nobility. Matters came to a head in the middle of his reign, when in 1607, during a parliamentary session, nobleman Mikołaj Zebrzydowski accused the king of attempting to destroy the Polish constitution. Though Catholic, Zebrzydowski was supported by Protestant nobles who had not been appointed to high positions. Soon, righteous anger led to outright revolt, which was put down at Guzów on July 7, 1607. But although Zygmunt effectively

5. The best accounts of this era in English are Daniel Stone's *The Polish-Lithuanian State, 1386–1795* (Seattle: University of Washington Press, 2001), 129–244, and Norman Davies' *God's Playground: A History of Poland, vol. 1: The Origins to 1795* (Oxford: Clarendon Press, 1981), 327–53.

6. See Stone, *The Polish-Lithuanian State*, 140.

won the day and accepted the apologies of the insurrectionists, for the remainder of his reign he had to contend with a more oppositional Diet.

Concurrent with the Zebrzydowski revolt was the Dmitry episode, where influential Jesuits, filled with the zeal of the Counter-Reformational spirit, egged on Lithuanian magnates to accept the story spun by a shadowy émigré named Dmitry, whereby he claimed to be son and heir to Ivan I, who had died in 1584. Dmitry's undertaking to convert to Catholicism convinced his newfound supporters that with his help they could secure a strong foothold to the east, and that mass conversion would follow on the heels of conquest. After the death of Tsar Boris Godunov in 1605, Dmitry led an invasion of Russia, supported by highly trained regiments, and as he progressed towards Moscow he was joined by Cossacks and the famine-stricken peasantry. Having taken Moscow, he was crowned Tsar, but the presence of Polish and Lithuanian advisors soon soured relations with his people and he was overthrown in a popular uprising. A second Dmitry would emerge a number of years later, and this time he involved Sweden in his attempts to secure the Russian crown.[7] Zygmunt's own son, Władysław, was proposed as a compromise candidate, which would see the young man converting to Russian Orthodoxy and returning to Russia western lands which had been annexed in recent conquests. However, Zygmunt had no wish to countenance such an agreement, claiming both the crown for himself and voicing his intention to annex western Russia. In the face of such a declaration, together with competing Swedish claims, Russian nobles recaptured Moscow and killed the second Dmitry. With the Russians embroiled in a war with Sweden, Władysław, with the aid of Hetman (Commander) Jan Karol Chodkiewicz and an army of Cossacks, was able to retain his power-base in western Russia and uphold his claim to the Russian throne.[8] Though Livonia was the principal flashpoint between Poland and Sweden, it was the decision of the Swedish king, Gustavus Adolphus, in 1626, to attack Royal Prussia that exposed Poland's tentative control of its borders to the west and northwest. By 1629, Poland had lost most of its coastline to the Swedes, who also went on to seize control of a demilitarized and weakened Gdańsk. The scene for a national disaster was set.

On the death of Zygmunt in 1632, the throne was awarded unopposed to his son, Władysław, but the new king failed to address the internal threat from the emerging power of the Cossacks, who had spent decades defending the Commonwealth's southern border from the slave raids of the Tartars. Having also provided a disciplined militia for Polish noblemen annexing vast tracts of land in

7. This episode was recounted by Hetman Stanisław Żółkiewski (1547–1620) in his memoir *Początek i progres wojny moskiewskiej* (Warsaw: Gebethner i Wolff, 1920). Żółkiewski led Polish troops into Moscow following his victory over combined Swedish and Russian forces in the Battle of Klushino.

8. See Leszek Podhorecki, *Jan Karol Chodkiewicz, 1560–1621* (Warsaw: Wydawnictwo Ministerstwa Obrony Narodowej, 1982), 238–43.

the Ukraine, the Cossacks began to demand more than simply mercenary status. This discontent was compounded by the grievances of the Orthodox population, who resented their poor treatment at the hands of the prejudiced and arrogant Polish magnates. The failure to tackle these festering issues came home to roost under the reign of his stepbrother, Jan II Kazimierz Waza (1648–1668), when a Cossack uprising broke out, led by Bohdan Chmielnicki. Aided by mercenary Turks and Tartars, who relished the opportunity to rape and plunder, the Cossacks ran amok and carried out the reduction of the peasant and Jewish populations in the Polish Ukraine. Although the Cossack rebellion was eventually put down, the Polish state was so weakened that it was unable to fend off Swedish armies that swept through the country as far as Kraków in the years 1655 to 1656, pillaging and wreaking destruction as they went. A reversal in Poland's fortunes occurred at the monastery of Jasna Góra in Częstochowa, where a small number of monks and local gentry withstood a month-long siege by the Swedes. Their success was accredited to the divine intervention of Mary, the Mother of God, and this perceived miracle gave rise to an enduring veneration of the Black Madonna image held in the monastery's main chapel. The small Swedish force would end up beating a hasty retreat northward, but came under constant attack from armed peasant militias. However, this war of attrition would continue for four more years and leave the country utterly devastated, with more than half the population dead. As a result of plague and wholesale slaughter, the cities were almost emptied, and bourgeois culture almost disappeared.[9] What is more, the vast tracts of land left empty were appropriated by corrupt and increasingly dissolute magnates and nobles, many of whom had gone over to the Swedish army but had then deftly re-switched loyalties when the tide had turned. Looking to deflect culpability, Poland's nobles made scapegoats out of the members of the Arian church, who in 1657 were given the choice of either conversion to Catholicism or banishment. To add to their litany of outrages, the magnates found a way of paralyzing the political system by their appropriation of the *Liberum Veto*, which upheld the tradition of unanimity at central and local assemblies.[10] Such was the chaotic nature of rule in the country at the time that bemused foreign powers observing from without soon labelled the governance of Poland as "The Anarchy," a term encapsulating a

9. As Czesław Miłosz notes, "The depressed condition of urban areas remained a constant factor in determining the direction of Polish cultural history for the next two centuries. The date 1655–1656 marked the end of bourgeois literature." *The History of Polish Literature* (Berkeley: University of California Press, 1983), 114.

10. As Norman Davies writes, "The Sejm, the dietines, and the Royal elections were all governed by the principle of unanimity. It seems incredible to the modern observer that such an ideal should have been taken seriously. But it was, and it formed the basis of all their proceedings. No proposal could become law, and no decision was binding, unless it received the full assent of all those persons who were competent to consider it. A single voice of dissent was equivalent to total rejection." *God's Playground*, 1:259.

state of affairs to which many historians have attributed the ultimate downfall of the Polish-Lithuanian Commonwealth.[11]

Anna Stanisławska's Early Life

Anna Stanisławska was born in 1651. Her father, Michał Stanisławski, was one of the heroes of his era, having distinguished himself as a soldier and in countless other roles in royal diplomacy and national politics.[12] He was not only Voivode (Governor) of Kiev, and a magnate with great wealth, but was also related to Poland's future king, Jan Sobieski (Sobieski's great aunt was Michał's grandmother). Stanisławska's mother was Krystyna Borkowa Szyszkowska, and her family had kindred links with both the powerful Potocki and Zebrzydowski families. By rights, Stanisławska should have had every expectation of a happy childhood, but death would take her mother when Stanisławska was only three years old, and not long after this, her father sent her to live with and be educated by the Dominican nuns in their cloister in Gródek near Kraków, where her great aunt on her mother's side, Gryzelda Dominika Zebrzydowska, was the prioress. Tragically, Gryzelda died following an outbreak of bubonic plague, and Stanisławska would never experience again anything approximating such motherly affection. In 1667, perhaps as a response to the recent death of Stanisławska's brother, Piotr, whom Stanisławska may possibly have never met, Michał took his daughter out of the convent and brought her home to the family estate of Maciejowice. Rapturous at the prospect, little did the young girl suspect that her being brought home was not inspired by sentiment, and that her father was not looking to make up for lost time.

A number of years previously, in 1663, Stanisławska's father had married again to Anna Potocka Kazanowska-Słuszka, a confidant of Jan Sobieski and a strong-willed woman who was determined to marry off her stepdaughter as soon as possible. Undoubtedly preoccupied with the turmoil in the country, Michał fell in readily with these plans[13] and found what should have been an ideal candidate for a son-in-law in the person of Jan Kazimierz Warszycki, son of Stanisław Warszycki from his first marriage to Helena Wiśniowiecka. Stanisław was Castellan of Kraków and a distinguished senator. As a magnate of great substance, he was

11. See Paweł Jasienica, *Polska anarchia* (Kraków: Wydawnictwo Literackie, 1988).

12. See Ida Kotowa, "Anna Stanisławska: pierwsza autorka polska," *Pamiętnik Literacki* 1–4 (1934): 267–68.

13. Concerning the issue of the forced marriage of young girls in seventeenth-century Poland, see Aleksander Brückner, *Dzieje kultury polskiej: Polska u szczytu potęgi*, vol. 2, 2nd ed. (Warsaw: Książka i Wiedza, 1958), 450–57; Zbigniew Kuchowicz, *Obyczaje staropolskie XVII–XVIII wieku* (Łódź: Wydawnictwo Łódzkie, 1974); Janusz Tazbir, *Studia nad kulturą staropolską* (Kraków: TAiWPN Universitas, 2001), 187–200.

also a church benefactor. Like Stanisławska's father, Stanisław Warszycki had earned a formidable reputation for military success and martial courage during the Swedish invasions.[14]

The Aesop Episode

Both fathers entered into negotiations and agreed terms, which anticipated the strengthening of bonds between the two great houses.[15] If Michał had heard any disturbing reports of the young man's mind and comportment, his failings must have been played down or explained away by Stanisław. Whatever of the regret that later followed, this marriage was principally a mercantile decision where factors of political influence and future income predominated, and this ill-considered bartering of his own daughter may have later gnawed at Michał's conscience, or at least that is what Stanisławska believed had been the case. Stanisławska, too, must have heard of Warszycki's aberrations and implored her father to release her from the arrangement. But bolstered by the determination of his new wife, Michał gave the heartfelt pleadings of his daughter no truck whatsoever.

Stanisławska's disquietude proved justified, for Jan Kazimierz was a monstrous-looking degenerate who feared only his father's chastisement and beatings, which were frequent and must have contributed inevitably to the young man's physical and psychological ailments.[16] Only ever referring to her husband by his real name on one occasion—which comes at the end of the episode as she bids him farewell and magnanimously wishes him well for the future—Stanisławska would give Jan Kazimierz the name of Aesop due to his exceptional ugliness and decrepit demeanor. The Aesop of Antiquity was invariably described as one of the ugliest men of his time,[17] and Stanisławska's very association with Aesop must have provided grist to her palpable disgust.

14. Kotowa, "Anna Stanisławska," 268–70.

15. Of marital negotiation in seventeenth-century Poland, Maria Bogucka writes, "Marriage was, as a rule, the outcome of negotiations conducted more by relatives or friends than by the interested parties themselves. [...] The date for the wedding was established after negotiations concerning dowry and jointure, and often among the more affluent nobility, burghers, and even rich peasants, following the signing of a detailed marriage contract." *The Lost World of the "Sarmatians": Custom as the Regulator of Polish Social Life in Early Modern Times* (Warsaw: Polish Academy of Sciences, Institute of History, 1996), 75–77.

16. As Zbigniew Kuchowicz writes, "młodzieniec, który przeszedł wychowanie domowe lub szkolne, doświadczył równocześnie na własnej skórze setek razów" [A young man who had been reared in the home or had attended school would have hundreds of marks on his skin to show for it]: *Obyczaje staropolskie*, 414. The harsh treatment of children in the noble households of seventeenth- and eighteenth-century Poland is also treated in Brückner, *Dzieje kultury polskiej*, 447–50.

17. The anonymously written *Vita Aesopi*, dating to the 1st or 2nd century CE, told many ribald tales of Aesop's life as the slave of his master Xynthus, and the stories proved so popular that they were

The wedding day, which took place sometime in spring, is depicted in the poem as a ghastly spectacle, with Aesop, chaperoned by a one-eyed priest, arriving in a carriage and declaring that he does not know why he has been brought there. But under the watchful and stern gaze of his father, the groom does his best to hide the irredeemable deficiencies in his character. Stanisławska paints the picture of a bride recoiling at absolutely everything connected with the celebration, but typical of an indomitable spirit that comes to the fore as the episode progresses, she tries to put a brave face on things and accepts Aesop's invitation to dance. But the guests have only the shortest of time to compliment the newlyweds gracing the floor, as Aesop abandons Stanisławska in mid-step and she has to be escorted back to her seat. The situation achieves comic proportions when the young couple are brought to the bridal chamber, where they are expected to consummate their union. Whatever the predilections of the groom, he proves incapable of going through with this marital rite and shows himself to be more concerned with squashing flies against the windowpane. Fortunately for Stanisławska, her attendant maidens had the good sense to whisk her away before any further shame could be heaped upon what should have been a sacred beginning. Stanisławska's father, who as a leader of men and presumably a good judge of character, realized that he had been greatly deceived as to both the suitability of the candidate for his daughter's hand, and to the conditions in which she would live, with it emerging soon after the wedding feast that her newly acquired father-in-law intended to live with the couple; although it may just be that Stanisław understandably wished to be present in the house in order to protect Stanisławska from his son.

Whenever Aesop had the run of the home, he was violent and cruel towards Stanisławska, and he seems to have settled on a strategy of hounding his wife to death. Stanisławska, in turn, could only hope against hope that her father would rescue her. Tragically for Stanisławska, her father took ill with dysentery on a military expedition and died in Podkamień[18] soon after, although this news was deliberately kept from her on the orders of Stanisławska's father-in-law, who feared that as an heiress to great wealth and lands, she might take action to free herself of her marital bond. From what Stanisławska relates, her father had already been considering options to extract his daughter from the world to which he had committed her, and before his death had appointed Jan Sobieski as Stanisławska's guardian. As Stanisławska was entangled in a dispute with her stepmother over inheritance rights, she was able to meet Sobieski under false pretences. During this meeting, Sobieski advised Stanisławska to mend bridges with her stepmother,

incorporated into other folkloric and poetic traditions. For a study on the Polish Aesopic tradition in the late Renaissance, see Janina Abramowska, *Polska bajka ezopowa* (Poznań: Wydawnictwo Naukowe UAM, 1991).

18. See Kotowa, "Anna Stanisławska," 270.

which entailed making magnanimous overtures to the very woman responsible for having put her in the position that she now found herself.

Although Stanisławska rails against the machinations of Fortune throughout her work, serendipity played its part when in June 1669, a royal election was held in Warsaw following the abdication of Jan II Kazimierz Waza, which brought the Waza dynasty to an end. Stanisławska coaxed her father-in-law into allowing her to join them in Warsaw, perhaps once again claiming that the protracted issues pertaining to her inheritance needed further resolution. Having positioned themselves at the very heart of the campaign to elect Michał Korybut Wiśniowiecki,[19] who was favored by many of the Polish nobility, the Warszyckis agreed to allow Stanisławska to reside in a nearby convent. Once inside the walls, Stanisławska claimed sanctuary, a move which was then supported by Sobieski, who as part of the faction of malcontents which had seen the defeat of their French candidate, Duke d'Enghien, for the kingship, threw all his support behind Stanisławska. It could not have been lost on Sobieski that his actions greatly discommoded and shamed a family that had singularly thwarted his ambitions.[20]

Free from the clutches of father and son, who planned stratagems to kidnap her, or worse, Stanisławska was free to instigate annulment proceedings. Sobieski appointed lawyers to represent Stanisławska, who argued that she had been married against her will. Witnesses were produced, but the testimony of her stepmother proved crucial. Magnanimously injuring her own reputation, Stanisławska's stepmother testified to the roles played by herself and her husband in forcing Stanisławska up the aisle, a testimony that tipped the scales in Stanisławska's favor and secured the judgment, which was later upheld by Rome. The divorce—for Stanisławska refers to the judgment as such—created quite a stir in the royal court and elsewhere, and in other times could have led to soul-searching in many quarters on the legality of arranged marriages had more been made of the reasons given for the annulment. But in spite of the fact that Stanisławska was made the subject of unsparing verses, which poked fun at her rather unusual status as maiden and divorcee,[21] the plight of Stanisławska was considered so extreme

19. At the election, Warszycki famously maintained that future parliaments should be held on horseback so as to safeguard the freedoms which their ancestors had won through bloody conflict. See Stone, *The Polish-Lithuanian State*, 233–34.

20. See Lajos Hopp, "Sobieski a orientacja profrancuska malkontentów węgierskich," in *Studia z dziejów epoki Jana III Sobieskiego*, ed. Krystyn Matwijowski et al. (Wrocław: Wydawnictwo Uniwersytetu Wrocławskiego, 1984), 47–62. See also Robert I. Frost, *After the Deluge. Poland-Lithuania and the Second Northern War, 1655–1660* (Cambridge: Cambridge University Press, 2003), 177–78. Little did Sobieski know at this time that the reign of Wiśniowiecki would be short: four years later, the incumbent died of acute food poisoning, which event paved the way for Sobieski's own election as king.

21. Morsztyn summed up the conundrum of Stanisławska's position following the divorce with the lines: "Pannam, bo męża nie znam, alem przecie żona, / Bo żyje ten, któremu była poślubiona" [A

that few paid attention to the legal technicalities upon which she had won her annulment. Freedom came at a price, however, as Stanisławska was ordered by the court to return a lengthy inventory of gifts which she had received, and her aggrieved ex in-laws made sure that every last trinket was returned.

Life after Aesop

Whilst Stanisławska was waiting out her time in the cloister, she received a proposal of marriage from Jan Oleśnicki, Sobieski's dashing chief cavalry officer and judge of Sandomierz; and a widower who was reputed to have poisoned his first wife. Even though she initially rejected his proposal of marriage, by the year's end, Oleśnicki had settled Stanisławska's debts and the two were married, but not before having had to secure a dispensation from Rome following the discovery that they were blood-related. There followed six years of connubial happiness, during which time they were of "two souls in one body / One heart" [*Dwie dusze w jednym ciele, / jedno serce*] (Threnody 39, stanza 355).[22] During this period, Oleśnicki accompanied King Sobieski into numerous battles against the Turks. In 1675, whilst on a military expedition, he fell gravely ill when cholera swept through the camp. Sobieski had Oleśnicki brought home to his family estate of Szczekarzowice, where he died soon after.

There followed for Stanisławska a period of great grief, but she was roused from her desolation when it transpired that Oleśnicki's father wanted his son to be interred in the family chapel located in the Monastery of the Holy Cross on the mountain of Łysa Góra. Stanisławska resisted this move and determined to have Oleśnicki interred in a church in Tarłów, the adornment of which both she and her husband had funded. More pain would follow for Stanisławska when Oleśnicki's surviving relatives made recourse to the courts in order to reclaim the estate and lands of Szczekarzowice.

Not long after Oleśnicki's death, Stanisławska found herself being determinedly courted by Jan Zbąski, the chamberlain of the Lublin region, whose cousin was Bishop of Warmia. Stocky and uncomely, and about ten years or so older than the woman whom he had set his heart on marrying, Jan called upon the likes of Sobieski and Stanisławska's own stepmother to persuade Stanisławska of the benefits of such a match. Fortunately for Zbąski, Stanisławska shared the same tastes as other noblewomen of the age and had a weak spot for the accoutrements of courtship; and seemingly, when she saw her fastidious suitor astride a horse, she

---

Maid, for she knows no husband, and yet a wife, / For he lives, he to whom she was married]. Cited in Brückner, "Wiersze zbieranej drużyny," 426.

22. For a descriptive account of courtship and marriage in seventeenth- and eighteenth-century Poland, see Alojzy Sajkowski, *Staropolska miłość: Z dawnych listów i pamiętników* (Poznań: Wydawnictwo Poznańskie, 1981).

was greatly impressed by the figure he cut.[23] Soon after, Stanisławska succumbed to his attentions and accepted his proposal of marriage.

These were bellicose times when the elite were being asked to make extraordinary sacrifices in defense of the homeland. And even to discount war, a mild illness could take a person from this world in an instant. In such a context, we may sympathize with a preparedness to marry again on the part of Stanisławska, who was still a young woman and capable of having children.

Their wedding took place in Warsaw in 1677 amid great pomp and festivity, although some voiced their disapproval of the fact that Stanisławska had not occasioned respect for her recently departed husband. The couple chose to live on Zbąski's estate of Kurów, between the cities of Puławy and Lublin, where they led quiet and serene lives. This period of felicity was only marred by Zbąski's decision, contrary to the wishes of his wife, to concede defeat to the Oleśnicki family in the legal dispute over the Szczekarzowice estate. But when she saw how upset he was over the entire affair, Stanisławska forgave him wholeheartedly.

When the Ottoman forces laid siege to Vienna in July 1683, Zbąski, who was still an active soldier in spite of his age, courageously followed King Sobieski into battle. Having lined up before the walls of Vienna, martial fervor got the better of him, and he charged out of the ranks only to be wounded in the leg by a musket bullet. Initially, the wound did not seem to be life-threatening, and the royal physician wrote to Stanisławska stating that her husband would return home soon. However, Zbąski's condition deteriorated rapidly and Stanisławska rushed to be by her dying husband's side. Tragically, Stanisławska had only made it as far as Kraków when news was brought to her that he had passed away. Stanisławska subsequently learned that it had been Zbąski's great hope to the very end that he would die in the arms of his beloved wife. Stanisławska would collapse from grief when shots were fired over his coffin.

Widowhood

The writing of *Orphan Girl* draws a line under Stanisławska's life up until that point. As the poet herself hinted at the beginning of the poem, life at the court of King Sobieski held no appeal and she preferred a solitary existence, alone with her memories and removed from all the pomp, fanfare, and intrigue of courtly life. That Stanisławska was indignant at the excesses of those who held wealth and power—with many of the transgressors hailing from the ranks of her own family and circle of friends and acquaintances—may be gleaned from the records of a contemporaneous court proceeding which tells how Stanisławska led a company of servants and local villagers against the home of overlords who had come into

23. Threnody 59, stanza 523: "Że na koniu dobrze siedział, / z tego mi się lepiej podobał" [That he sat well on a horse, / and that pleased me more].

the possession of a neighboring estate arising from an unpaid debt. When later called before a court in Lublin, Stanisławska had to answer the charge of having hurled invectives against the lady of the house.[24]

Towards the end of her life, Stanisławska donated generously to both the Piarist monks of Dunajgród and missionary orders in both Lublin and Warsaw. Her family must have had foreknowledge of her intention to divest more of her wealth in favor of the religious orders, because they made their objections known in no uncertain terms. But Stanisławska remained fixed on her course of action. In her final days she was cared for in the home of a Jewish woman in the town of Kurów. In great pain, she had her last will and testament witnessed by a local bailiff, who delivered both the will and the deeds of her properties to Fr. Michał Bartłomiej Tarło, the cousin of her third husband. Stanisławska had left her entire estate of Maciejowice to the Piarist order, and one of the three surviving portraits made of her in the latter stages of her life makes mention of her patronage. Anna Stanisławska-Zbąska died on June 2, 1701, and it seems that the tumult of her life continued in the wake of her death. Her testament was contested by her direct heir, Jan Koniecpolski, which led to protracted litigation between the plaintiff and the missionary order.[25]

The Writing of Orphan Girl

Having settled affairs pertaining to the protection of her estate, and with time and the heart to devote to such an undertaking, in 1685, Stanisławska began to commit to verse the vicissitudes of her life up to the death of her third husband. The prospective poet must have considered that her time on this earth, blighted as it had been with misfortune and mishap, contained many incidents and episodes worthy of an epic account. As Stanisławska writes in the end poem to readers, a flood of memories had returned. And so, there surely must also have been a therapeutic dimension to the exercise.[26]

Stanisławska may even have been inspired in her work by Anna Potocka-Stanisławska, her stepmother, who had encouraged Katarzyna Siemiotkowska[27] several years earlier to pen a collection of poems entitled *Gospodarskie*

24. See Kotowa, "Anna Stanisławska," 274.

25. See Kotowa, "Anna Stanisławska, 276–77.

26. Many commentators regard the poem as being part of a cathartic process whereby Stanisławska came to terms with the grief caused by *Fortuna variabilis*. See Ursula Phillips, "Piszące białogłowy od średniowiecza do końca XVIII wieku," in *Pisarki polskie od średniowiecza do współczesności: przewodnik*, ed. Grażyna Borkowska, Małgorzata Czermińska, and Ursula Phillips (Gdańsk: Wydawnictwo Słowo/Obraz Terytoria, 2000), 5–16.

27. See Tadeusz Mikulski, "Drobiazgi Staropolskie: Anna Zbąska ze Stanisławskich," *Ruch Literacki* 7–8 (1935): 202–3.

nabożeństwo [The Arcadian Mass], a series of reworked devotional morning and evening prayers, which were appropriately dedicated to Stanisławska-Potocka. In fact, Siemiotkowska could be said to have a claim on the anachronistic title that has been traditionally accredited to Anna Stanisławska as that of Poland's first woman author.[28]

Featured in the title itself, the word "treny," meaning "threnodies" or "laments," identifies the work closely with Jan Kochanowski's collection of the same name. Just as Kochanowski, writing one hundred years earlier, had upbraided Fortune and pagan Classical personifications of Death following the loss of his infant child, so too does Stanisławska rage against the fates throughout the work for their having treated her so shamefully. The role of Fortune had held a fascination for writers and philosophers from the time of ancient Greece right up to the late Renaissance, with many perceiving Fortune as cruel and malicious, playing some high-handed game and shuffling doubtful benefits. Stanisławska's view of Fortune aligned itself closely with Horace's contention that the attainment of happiness was being constantly thwarted by Fortune's malice, and that there was very little that could be done to alter matters. However, Stanisławska's interpretation of Fortune was inextricably linked to her own experience, wherein she accepted that Fortune would always do its worst and that the only appropriate response was to determinedly "face Chance down," all the while finding comfort and strength in prayer.[29] Aside from this repeated invocation to Fortune, it is thought that beyond the scattering of Biblical illusions, the work is taken principally from life. And indeed, it was the adversarial nature of Stanisławska's life, filled as it was with the drama of courtroom appearances and the realities and consequences of war, which must have honed her power of observation and endowed her with a barbed and cutting wit. Stanisławska's failure to pursue publication of the poem is puzzling, especially given that the work often addresses readers directly, which indicates an aspiration that the work be published and read. Indeed, in the opening poem, readers are asked to set aside any prejudice about her sex, whereas elsewhere

28. There were, of course, other women writers in pre-Baroque Poland, such as the Reform-minded Regina Filipowska and Zofia Oleśnicka, both of whom flourished in the mid-sixteenth century and who wrote Protestant religious hymns. We must also mention Anna Memorata, who penned the Latin *Carmen gratulatorium*. Born in Leszno in the early seventeenth century, Memorata was the daughter of a pastor to Czech Brethren. In spite of her Bohemian origins, she signed her name as *virgo polona*. See Kotowa, "Anna Stanisławska," 286–88; Rott, *Kobieta z przemalowanego portretu*, 11–30; and Maya Peretz, "In Search of the First Polish Woman Author," *The Polish Review* 38, no. 4 (1993): 481.

29. Stanisławska's determination to resist the slings and arrows of misfortune through positive action distinguishes her belief system from the Stoic outlook. See Halina Popławska, "'Żałosne treny' Anny Stanisławskiej," in *Pisarki polskie epok dawnych*, ed. Krystyna Stasiewicz (Olsztyn: Wyższa Szkoła Pedagogiczna, 1998), 89–111. For a discussion on the perception and depiction of Fortune in Renaissance and Baroque Poland, see Jacek Sokolski, *Bogini, pojęcie, demon: Fortuna w dziełach autorów staropolskich* (Wrocław: Wydawnictwo Uniwersytetu Wrocławskiego, 1996).

the work is strewn with homespun advice to young people: albeit Stanisławska's idea of a successful marriage, based on mutual fondness and sound finances, was perhaps, ironically, not far from the criteria averred to by her own father when he was negotiating the match with Aesop. Peculiar to the poetry of *Orphan Girl* are emotional and psychological states brought to life in snapshot moments of time that are brimming with humor and sardonic tones. The many political and historical upheavals of the day only receive a precursory mention, and if they do so at all, only feature when they impact upon Stanisławska's life directly.

More frequently still, Stanisławska directly appeals to readers for their sympathy as she relates a time or episode which brought her acute pain or despair. And so, it is reasonable to contend that Stanisławska may not have written *Orphan Girl* simply for cathartic reasons but that the work's artistic and biographical imperatives could only have been fulfilled by the anticipation of a readership.[30] One possible explanation for the work not seeing the light of day is that Stanisławska, on completing the work, changed her mind about publication for fear of offending the Warszycki and Oleśnicki families. One way or another, just as Stanisławska's hopes and dreams were so often thwarted in life, her presumably tentative hopes for literary posterity were also dealt a blow by unforeseeable circumstances.

That the work disappeared for more than two hundred years is all the more tragic as the rigors of the poetic strictures that Stanisławska had ascribed to the writing of the poem betray a highly tuned artistic ambition not common for this era.[31] Stanisławska chose for the poem's versification short octosyllabic octaves with *aabb* grammatical rhymes, often referred to as Częstochovian rhymes and regarded with derision in Poland because of their perceived simplicity and banality.[32] And yet, it could be said that Stanisławska's decision to place her life's story within this unusual poetic framework reflected her own tenacious personality, characterized as it was by a determination to resist always the confinements of tradition and the expectations of others. It has been suggested that for "The Aesop Episode" in particular, Stanisławska may have drawn upon the farcical comedies which she

30. See Alfred Fei, "Z poezji staropolskiej: Jan Smolik – Anna Stanisławska," *Pamiętnik Literacki* 1–4 (1936): 815–40. See also Karolina Targosz, *Sawantki w Polsce XVII wieku: Aspiracje intelektualne kobiet ze środowisk dworskich* (Warsaw: Retro-Art, 1997).

31. See Jan Stanisław Bystroń, *Dzieje obyczajów w dawnej Polsce: wiek XVI–XVIII*, vol. 1, 2nd ed. (Warsaw: Państwowy Instytut Wydawniczy, 1976), 391–92. See also Tadeusz Bieńkowski, "Panegiryk a życie literackie w Polsce XVI i XVII wieku," in *Z dziejów życia literackiego w Polsce XVI i XVII wieku*, ed. Hanna Dziechcińska (Wrocław: Zakład Narodowy im. Ossolińskich, 1980), 183–96.

32. Alfred Fei could not ascribe to Stanisławska's epic the status of a literary work, criticizing in particular the fact that she had failed to draw inspiration from any of her literary contemporaries. See Fei, "Z poezji staropolskiej," 838. That said, Zdzisław Stieber noted numerous rhymes which were used by poets such as Wacław Potocki and Piotr Kochanowski, who drew on poetic traditions of the Sandomierz region. See Stieber, "Przyczynki do historii polskich rymów, 1. Rymy sandomierskie XVI i XVII wieku," *Język Polski* 3 (1950): 110–13.

which she would have seen in courtly theater.[33] It is certainly an explanation that would give credence to the notion that the poet's entire ambition for the poem was that it would be a performable work that could excite both high laughter and salty tears in equal measure.[34]

An Other Voice: A Note on the Translation

My translation is based on Kotowa's 1935 edition. Given that the power of the account is predicated on the poetic form in which it was conceived, I looked to emulate the metrical and rhyming scheme of the poem and also to accentuate its rhetorical and performative potential. The poem presented here is a verse translation and has strived to serve what I regard as the poem's narrational imperative. I took this judgment further and divided "The Aesop Episode" into smaller titled episodes, which is a step intended to extol the poem's epic and historical sweep and also to support the reading of what is a lengthy poem.

I would be greatly amiss if I did not make some mention here of the margin notes. Very often, I incorporated information from a given margin note into the accompanying stanza, and because of this, I was strongly tempted to do away with the margin notes altogether. But in the interests of preserving the entirety of the text, I decided not to do so. However, it is important to be cognizant of the fact that the notes are intended to be contemporaneous explanations of past events, and so, for example, Sobieski is given the title throughout as "His Majesty the King." This is because he was king at the time of Stanisławska's writing of the poem, but in the events that the poem describes, Sobieski's coronation was some way off. What is more, where Stanisław Warszycki is mostly referred to as "the old man" in the poem proper, in the margin notes, Stanisławska refers to him as "Master Krakowski," which alludes to his link with Kraków. Adding more to the confusion is the fact that Jan Kazimierz Warszycki, or Aesop, is given the name of "kasztelanic" in the margin notes, which is a diminutive form of "castellan," suggesting that he is the son of the Castellan. And so, in the translated margin notes Aesop appears almost exclusively as "the Castellan's son."

My translation ends at the point where Stanisławska claims her freedom from Aesop and is looking forward with some trepidation to the next chapter in her life. Two further episodes—or marriages, as the case may be—await translation.

33. See Targosz, *Sawantki w Polsce*, 302.

34. Hanna Dziechcińska has written extensively on women's writing, theater and performable art in Poland during this era: see her (in order of date of publication) *Literatura a zabawa: Z dziejów kultury literackiej w dawnej Polsce* (Warsaw: Państwowe Wydawnictwo Naukowe, 1981); *Kultura literacka w Polsce XVI i XVII wieku* (Warsaw: Wydawnictwo Naukowe Semper, 1994); and *Ciało, strój, gest w czasach saskich renesansu i baroku* (Warsaw: Wydawnictwo Naukowe Semper, 1996).

This translation could not have been completed without drawing on the research which has been written on *Orphan Girl*, and it is certainly my hope that "The Aesop Episode" celebrates not only the legacy of the work itself but also the work of the many scholars who have thrown light on the ways and means by which the poet came to relate both her life's story and the sufferings of her age.

Jesus, Mary and Joseph

ANNA STANISŁAWSKA

Orphan Girl

A Transaction, or an Account of the Entire Life
of an Orphan Girl by way of Plaintful Threnodies
in the Year 1685

The Aesop Episode

To the Reader

The title may just leave you scratching your head,
Wondering how it is that I sing of my death.
But life, you see, is a series of threnodies,
And threnodies spring from life's cruel veil of tears.
I contend that we should sing of certitudes:
That life will always swipe the legs from under us.
Just to look back on the years that you have had,
Will have you losing count of the tears you have shed.
What is more, I'll argue that any contentment
You enjoyed was but a briefly snatched moment.
I'd like you to know what I've come to realise:
That Time is no healer deserving of praise.
I am one of those whose dreams have been thwarted,
And having seen Fortune ply its ruthless trade,
I can speak about lives robbed of happiness.
So heed my words and listen to my advice:
Face with courage the capricious ways of Chance,
For life only brings a mixed bag of highs and lows.
Now that I've said my piece, if this work's not for you,
With all its shortcomings, perhaps you should know
That it's been penned by one of the fairer sex.
Let your good self press on, indulge me in this.

A PREAMBLE OF DOLOR

Threnody I

1.
Favor me, Lord, upon my road,
For it may come to pass that dread
Takes hold, traipsing this chosen way:
See to it my steps do not stray!
I shall run to far-flung places,
Where I just may unearth, perhaps,
Some comfort for my sorry heart,
Which grief has left hard-pressed.

Here I seek contentment for my broken heart, wanting to take several paths.

2.
I shall not wade to the far side
Of the Danube, for a sharp sword
Pierced the heart not so long ago.
Why should I cross this river now?
It is clear these humming waters
Will bring me none of their coolness.
So you will just have to be content
With your river-share of water nymphs.

I fear the Danube, fearing the sorrow felt when my husband died before the walls of Vienna.

3.
So I go to the fragrant gardens:
But here, too, all seems hopeless,
For neither can the sweet odor
Nor the flowering riot of color
Offer me any consolation.
I have long ceased to love such things:
The nightingale, with its soft cry,
Is but for me a pitch too high.

Where I once found contentment, never will I now have consolation.

4.
I am now in a green meadow
Amongst herbs of sweet aroma.
They provide me with some relief
And rest from my trouble and grief.
But even here, the pleasant zephyrs
Have taken a turn for the worse.
So in place of a pleasant breeze,
I'm out of sorts and ill at ease.

5.
And then an idea comes to mind,
That the revelry I may find
At court, with all its lofty talk,
May lighten my gloom-filled spirit.
But what for me its dainty treats,
What attraction could taste so sweet?
I have the warning: and I'll give
It to whoever wants this life.

6.
So I go into the deep forest
And cry for all that's been lost.
I relive such experiences
That barely warrant repeating.
Which fine leafy trees shall provide
Me with sorely-needed shade?
Here I think on hopes gone astray,
Lost in a world awhirl with glee.

Making my way through the vast forest, I choose to rest under the cross of the family coat of arms.

7.
But even here my thoughts do stray,
Giving me great cause for dismay.
I should not sit under this tree,
Where man's last day of pure gaiety
Came with his first pleasured moment—
Lost forever that very instant.
So though I give all trees short shrift,
Beneath these boughs I choose to rest.

8.
Here I'll sit, all safe and secure;
        And sit I do, with grace and care.
Though this tree grows a most vile fruit,
        He who first savored its taste
Sets about making for me here
        A fine drink, full of sweet flavor.
And I, who have already tasted
        Of this fruit, can hardly resist.

THE HURTS OF CHILDHOOD

Threnody II

9.
Not three years old, but six months shy,
Did I step into a life turned sour:
Our mother's death left us orphans.
There's been no letup ever since.
There we were, just little children
And contending with affliction:
My brother and I had to cope
With a grief that left us no hope.

The crest of the one-third cross also brought years of troubles, for facing me was the loss of my mother.

10.
I pass over the transactions
Of my life which playful Fortune's
Placed in my path, like a comedy
Giving purpose to adversity.
Fate had dealings with my father,
Who paid me well for this bother:
Putting me in amongst the nuns—
I learnt patience at a young age.

The transactions of my life.

11.
And there, and in a hidden room,
I would receive my upbringing;
Being reared by the good sisters.
Though affliction came, as it does;
Their prayers on my behalf almost
Saw me offering up my ghost.
And so, though sick and in their care,
All they did was send me elsewhere.

When living in the cloister, I almost died of pox.

12.
Yet the heavens in their goodness,
Knowing what a young person needs,
Provided me with a guardian
Who was of my mother's bloodline.
Great was the kindred affection
And most sincere was the minding,
But sadly it would come to pass
That jealous fate begrudged me this.

Zebrzydowski, my grandfather, the Voivode of Kraków, looked after me, I was less than pleased.

13.
A time came when the cloister
Would hold me no more, my father
Having arranged for me to leave.
I couldn't get away soon enough,
Especially as the heavens
Had given in a mother's place
One who'd wipe away this orphan's
Tears with motherly affection.

Father delivers me from the cloister, having married my stepmother.

14.
But it has been explained to me
By someone of great certainty,
That it is hard to love a child
That you've not brought into this world.
Here I agree, it must be said,
And I'll go so far as to add,
That love will travel the distance
When the finances make sound sense.

VEXATION AT THE FATES

Threnody III

15.
Have you finished toying with me
Yet, O Fate, with your wicked ploys,
Abusing your slave like some sick joke.
But I see you're tightening the yoke—
You've stripped my brother of his youth,
Not allowing him life in this world.
So complete is your destruction,
My fallen home's a standing ruin.

The death of my brother, following which the family line ended.

16.
But how the biting twists of fate
Have turned to happiness of late!
Let the fates deal destiny's hand—
I am sure the cards will be kind.
May I relish these coming years,
As the world before me unfurls.
I shall treasure every moment,
And live life as it should be spent.

My maidenly state.

17.
O Fortune, be kind if you can!
You like, I discern, a situation
Where you bring hurt and then solace.
Yet, I ask you to hear these prayers:
Spare me the bondage of love,
For the fine years of my youth have
Still to run. As for freedom—now
That is a prize you could bestow.

I wish for no such resolution.

18.
Even when your treachery strikes,
You still reveal your friendly face.
And I am persuaded in this
By one who states with confidence
That it's far better for the young
To be locked into a coupling.
And indeed, more often than not,
This is how you settle our fate.

The persuasions of Fortune.

19.
I followed the advice you gave,
Not knowing that you would deceive
Me the way Laban did Jacob.
Such was your each and every step,
So I, who served you seven years,
Enduring pain and misery,
Can now cast a cold eye on things,
And recall the ill-fated twists.

20.
Leah, and not Rachel, was given
By stealth to Jacob by Laban.
He'd not given service for her
But set his sights on beauty's lure.
It is normal to desire gold,
To run far from the sight of mud.
Beauty's what we wish to behold.
We would all have that if we could.

21.
Such were your most capricious ways,
You placed beauty before my eyes,
With joyous scenes swirling through my head.
But you gave me Aesop instead.
Known for being extremely polite,
His manners were a true delight.
Was he born amongst the tigers?
Did he traipse trails with the bears?

Other handsome suitors had flattered me with their attentions, but I was given the son of the Castellan of Kraków, who had the looks of Aesop.

22.
For this prize I'll even the score,
  I will serve you for free, I swear.
This payment was never my wish,
  I did not seek this kind of loss.
Let him be content enough
  With pleasures he can give himself.
Lampart would happily make do
  With his very own house-trained doe.

I had no wish to marry him.

Lampart is a pig who pleasures himself.

I AM TO MARRY INTO A HOUSE OF DEVIANTS

Threnody IV

23.
You're now lashing out with your tongue,
Boldly splashing treacherous venom,
Bringing vexation to the hearts
Of my parents, whose bitter words
And taunts have, like shards of iron,
Pierced my heart. It is all unknown:
Some days they are just unpleasant;
On others, my father is kind.

My father was angry with me.

24.
You must have set your sights most high,
With heaven being your sole desire.
Are not the blessings of heaven
Best felt with a father's sanction?
We may surmise that Aesop's gifts
Failed to secure any bequest
From his father, who gave his wife
All things, and made his son a slave.

Threnody V

25.
The wedding is fast approaching,
The articles are being written.
Melancholy and great sadness
Have me feeling weak and feverish.
My head is filled with thoughts of death,
With thoughts of escaping this fate.
Many think that I should be pleased
To be planning my wedding feast.

The wedding day was announced, and from melancholy I fell into a feverish state.

26.
My father is far from cheery
When he pens me in a corner
And speaks words of great passion:
"You, my only daughter, my own
Flesh and blood, are trying very hard
To shatter my sorely-tried heart.
Rid yourself of girlish regret
And submit to the plans I've made!"

My perturbed father speaks with me.

27.
I am not spared a verbal lashing
From the mistress, with her saying
That nothing can be done at this stage,
And that I'll grow to love my leash:
"It's no use you crying these tears,
And whining will get you nowhere.
You'll not find in your father's eye
A hint of concern for his child."

My stepmother pleads with me, threatening me with the displeasure of my father.

28.
And so, I pluck up the courage
To speak to Father of my plight,
Hoping against hope that he may
Just feel some pity for his prey.
I fall to my knees, so saying:
"I'm ready to do your bidding.
Just think well here on what you have,
Or you'll be seeing me in the grave."

I mustered the courage to speak to my father.

29.
Clearly moved by my spoken fears,
        My father's eyes now fill with tears.
And he says in a gentle voice:
        "I'd sooner kill the animals
Of the forest than act against
        My beloved daughter's interests.
I've spoken true, so hear me now:
        You'll do what your father tells you!

My father speaks to me with sorrow.

30.
If tyranny's the stock and trade
        Of your father-in-law, you'll not
Have to live under the man's roof.
        You can always come here to live.
Just think of the lands and forests
        That'll be yours. All the trees and beasts.
And where things seem unbearable,
        Riches will make up the shortfall.

31.
You'll have all sorts of independence,
        And as Lady you'll have servants.
Once again, I say, not a hair
        Of yours will be touched. Have no fear.
Bring your new husband to our hearth—
        Before all ye'll both play your part.
I shall embrace him like a son—
        This man I'll take under my wing."

32.
There's no hope for a solution.
        So snared by wily Fortune,
My future is anyone's guess.
        So, Father, I'll submit to this,
Your will. Though I know that one day
        A father's heart will break to see
His child, a prisoner in bonds,
        Shackled to a monstrous husband.

I give him my answer.

33.
My father becomes most nervous
About my health, and he takes steps
To fetch eminent physicians
To my bedside. A fine surgeon
Declares that fevers must be bled,
So he makes my arms flow with blood.
Following this, though left half-spent,
I do note some returning strength.

Steps are taken to restore my health.

34.
Hardly on my feet once again,
We are busy about the town,
A place of councils and debates.
But I will not wed in this place,
For it's only right that this shame
Takes place secretly in my home.
When your husband's a laughing stock,
Best keep the key and turn the lock.

We depart from Warsaw.

THE WEDDING

Threnody VI

35.
Three days pass and guests from both sides
	Converge and exchange niceties.
From the wrong side is a go-between,
	Who is blind from what I discern,
Sent ahead by Aesop to march
	Me up to the door of the church.
But my father is just livid:
	"The groom must come and fetch his bride!"

The Castellan's son sends a messenger to bring me to the church. My father does not agree.

36.
When Aesop enters the courtyard,
	My family rushes out to bid
Him welcome. He looks like a gander
	Peering out the carriage window.
He barely bows to my father;
	With the rest he doesn't bother.
They're pulling me by my dress
	And pushing me towards... This!

37.
O heart, what it was like back then
	As we struggle to recall the pain?
Had you thought our youth would ever
	Be sold down that sorry river?
O Death, you should have struck me down
	When you first pondered the notion
Of slitting my neck with your scythe.
	How is it that this wretch still lives?

My sorrow.

38.
Here now at the altar I stand,
And why, I'm asking, have you bound
My temple with a golden wreath?
Let all and sundry here behold
The blushing groom and red-faced bride.
What a coupling for Nature's pride!—
He with his overgrown moustache,
She with a crane's neck that looks stretched.

39.
The Bishop binds our hands with his stole.
Oh, how my heart jolts and recoils
At the sight of my companion:
The ugliest man it's ever seen!
He hardly knows what's going on here,
For the oath's being whispered in his ear
By someone who has been ordered
To whisper each and every word.

The wedding.

40.
As he himself declares aloud:
"I knew nothing at all about
Where we were going to today,
Or why we were taking this journey.
And I never thought I'd enter
The chamber to see this picture
Of an angel.You're temptation
Itself, my delectable Anna!"

He said later that he did not know why he had made the journey, he understood that I was either an angel or a devil.

41.
The Bishop now duly proceeds
To the Rite of Marriage and reads
Vows which we're expected to take.
Here I'm given a severe look
From my father, seeing my silence
And the beseeching of my eyes.
He looks to Her, who is behind
My terrible predicament.

My father was irritated that I had no wish to speak.

42.
She who was most harsh with her words,
        Threatening me with my father's
Retribution, said that if I made
        Any fuss at all on the day
I would bitterly regret it:
        "Speak up!—do what you know is best!
I love you with a mother's heart,
        So think on this and play your part!"

My stepmother persuades me.

43.
The days of my bondage begin;
        A bondage I have not chosen.
My sad silence is all that's left.
        Indeed, there's little to be said.
And now shrill music fills the air,
        Greeting my fall through the trap door.
The wedding guests now take their seats
        And brace themselves for the speeches.

THE WEDDING BANQUET AND LATER

Threnody VII

44.
The chattering guests fall silent
As the great speaker makes to stand
And deliver his oration.
Though offense he'll give someone,
Few can match his abilities—
Even the senators grant him this.
And whenever he's in full flow,
It's all a pleasure to the ear.

I am given away by Rej, the Voivode of Lublin.

45.
Though sparing with each chosen phrase,
He looks to strike the right balance.
He gives due to the families,
Not to mention the dignitaries.
He heaps praise upon us maidens
And upon all our great customs,
Which puts the icing on the hour
With sumptuous lashings of honor.

46.
Oh, but what a pitiful sight
It was to see the great Voivode
Gushing like a tortured wretch.
Even a fool with a wise speech
Has some hold over his audience.
He stands to speak and all must listen.
How he takes it all in his stride,
Scanning a room where none can hide.

47.
The priest then praises the young man—
I'd call his sense into question!
Before us, a man of the cloth,
A man who serves the Lord. But
Instead of a priest's godliness,
He's busy counting properties:
All the churches that he will build;
All the hospitals he will fund.

The priest thanks me on behalf of the Castellan's son.

Threnody VIII

48.
It's time for us to take our places,
And the guests are shown to their seats.
This is when his father stands up
And lets it be known that Aesop
Will not be a cause of distress
To those who stand in his presence.
He'll shake his cap and let him know
When it's fitting for him to bow.

His father assigned him a servant, who stood in front of him and signalled with a cap whether to bow or drink: he was to act depending on its position.

49.
He is showing great obedience,
For he does not allow his gaze
To go wandering here and there.
He knows that he must take great care.
It concerns the skin on his back,
Being the son of a man so strict.
When someone tries to engage him,
He pretends he does not see them.

50.
We are all told to eat and drink,
But he is warned, being very drunk,
Not to keep swilling back the wine—
The horrors he'll face are made plain.
A father stands, he coughs and sighs,
A son sits, he but laughs and smiles.
The wretch doesn't know why he's laughing—
He asks himself this very question.

They were at cross-purposes.

51.
They are putting aside the chairs
And are preparing for the dance.
Having been told to act his role,
He is truly a sight to behold.
He could be a jester on stage,
Dancing as he is in his delia.
He's a man too small for dancing;
More a partridge that likes prancing.

52.
I am treated to many a turn,
As he swirls me about the room.
And the dancers pay their respects,
Praising the couple's best efforts.
But we've not yet finished the set,
When all of a sudden I'm left
By him twirling and abandoned.
Someone walks me back to my seat.

Having taken me up to dance, he left me alone in the middle of the chamber.

53.
My father can see his defects,
But he pretends not to notice.
He makes his way out of the room,
Only to come back in a short time.
Here the guests all rise to their feet
And leave the room in candlelight,
Leading me, as custom dictates,
To the table beside our bed.

54.
Aesop also winces at the sight
Before us, as he chews on a sweet
That's been maturing in some cell
For a year—it's a telling smell.
He's not happy but keeps chewing,
As my stepmother eggs him on:
She fills his ears with whispers,
She jabs his ribs with her fingers.

He offers sweets in the bridal chamber.

55.
They do not tarry long to dance,
And are going back to their rooms.
An old lady whispers something,
Sending him in our direction.
But he, having nodded his head,
Feels that little needs to be said.
You could hardly call it a bow—
It was but a nod, slightly low.

Lady Krakowska's maid whispered something to him.

56.
And the next day, after breakfast,
    I am getting myself dressed
When the ladies persuade Aesop,
    With a big push, to step up
To the task. On entering my chamber,
    He wipes the dust with his finger.
They say something, but the deaf man
    Is squashing flies against the pane.

In my chamber.

THE OLD MAN'S TERMS

Threnody IX

57.
They are regaling us with treats,
        And we sit down to the presents.
Surely I will receive something
        Special from the pleased-as-Punch groom.
But he quite takes me by surprise
        When he gives me a pearl necklace
Inherited from his grandmother.
        It's a necklace like no other.

They give gifts.

58.
It's truly something to behold,
        Like ulcers fashioned from gold.
And if you've the keenest of eyes,
        You may just make out the sparkles.
For this you would get three the same,
        Though surely not as nice as this one.
I will say this much of his gifts:
        They were all of a similar worth.

59.
The guests who've chosen to linger
        Often like to dance after dinner.
On occasion, Aesop tries a step,
        Dancing with his hand on his belt.
And she whom I must call mother,
        The loving wife of my father,
Does her best to find a moment
        With the begetter of this deviant.

60.
In order to hammer out terms
With some finely chosen words,
She says: "I'd like to say, well done
On the marriage of your fine son!
You must feel truly blessed
To have witnessed such happiness.
May the Lord our God bless them both,
And may children be their reward.

My stepmother tries to come to an understanding with Master Krakowski: what does he think will happen when, as promised, he hands over the estate to us?

61.
What the young couple need, for sure,
Is all the blessings of heaven's store.
And now I broach a delicate
Matter, and heed me you should,
As you take them under your wing.
Be mindful of what you have sworn,
And endow them with your substance.
They will know your benevolence.

62.
It was set down in the contract;
Remember, a pact is a pact.
You're beholden to everything
That ye fathers both settled on!"
And here the old man says, "Thank you"
For doing their best in all they do.
These words came as a great surprise,
As nothing here warranted praise.

63.
It is all brought out in the open
When he tells us of his great plan:
"They'll both be staying under my roof,
And whatever they want they'll have.
Their every wish will be my desire.
I will know the 'what' and the 'where,'
So there is no cause for unease.
All arrangements are sure to please.

He revealed that he would not yield the property to us.

64.
Don't worry, I can assure you
 That luxury is all they'll know.
Service at the snap of their fingers,
 They'll be smiling from ear to ear.
I myself will see to everything.
 They need only observe and learn,
So when the suitable time comes,
 They'll be sure-handed with the reins."

65.
Having heard all he had to say,
 She goes with this to my father
And apprises him of the situation,
 Advising he use persuasion:
"Do not fret, but offer counsel
 To your daughter on this betrayal.
The old man has revealed his hand.
 This was always his hidden plan.

She told this to my father.

66.
These were not the terms of the pact.
 What of the marital contract!?
He does not want to keep his word,
 But wants to be their overlord,
With them taking scraps from his hand
 Like two peasants on borrowed land.
If you intend to act, act now!
 Before he spirits them away."

67.
At this point, my father sees red.
 His serene face becomes twisted.
He loses the run of his speech.
 Gentle tones turn to a pitched screech:
"I swear by the heavens above,
 That I'll not be made a fool of.
If it is the last thing I do,
 I shall compel him to give way!

My father was greatly angered.

68.
He made his obligations plain,
Promising he'd give them free rein
Over their estate and affairs.
Did he not say he would steer clear!"
Knowing delay is not an option,
My father tackles things head on.
He fetches the priest with one eye,
And then bellows: "I'm ready to die!

69.
Get thee to that master of yours!
Tell him the word he gave is his!
I would sooner have him a corpse,
Turning and twisting in his grave,
Than entrust my precious daughter
To him to make her a beggar.
A fool-husband is bad enough,
Without him under the same roof!"

He sends the priest to Master Krakowski.

70.
Looking to smooth over the cracks,
The priest so says: "Hold all axes!
I understand how his mind works:
This is bluff with no winning cards.
Allow me what lies in my gift:
I have the means to heal this rift!
I'll tell him your depth of feelings,
How he has slapped you in the face."

The priests looks to persuade him.

71.
So the priest seeks out the old man,
Who can see by the priest's pale skin,
His sweating brow and worried eye,
That matters have not gone his way.
The priest then proceeds to relate
The charge my stepmother has made:
"She talks of a broken promise.
You should not have revealed your plans.

He tells Master Krakowski.

72.
I stood there in abject terror,
        Facing the rage of her father.
He says he'd gladly meet death,
        And that he'd sooner see you dead.
Shoot not the messenger for this.
        I humbly beg your forgiveness.
It was by heaven's providence
        That I escaped the man's clutches."

73.
The old man is also incensed.
        Each and every wrinkle is scrunched.
He directs his anger towards
        That busybody, and asserts:
"I know my worth, and I will not
        Yield to the demands of that lot.
I did not give my son in marriage
        For them to sling mud in my face."

Master Krakowski gets angry.

74.
Wanting to stem this flow of words,
        The priest makes habitual recourse
To the sycophant's stock and trade,
        So saying: "It's commonly declared
By all that you're a man of power.
        Believe what I say, and be sure
That men hold your word in great store.
        As for me, I couldn't agree more."

75.
He stops the priest in full flight
        And sends him scurrying from his sight
With the well-aimed fling of a stick.
        "That will teach him not to match-make!"
My father also gives him a cold eye,
        Being what he is, their little toy.
And that's where both parties choose
        To leave the matter—with silence.

He lunged at the priest with a stick, and the priest fled the room.

76.
Aesop is now going off to bed,
        And by a woman he's being led,
Who urges him to "Speak to her!"
        And he to this: "Whatever for?"
She whispers softly in his ear,
        But he doesn't seem to hear.
Having failed in her persuasions,
        She follows him out of the room.

The maid pleaded with him to ask for me.

THE FIRST DAYS OF MY BONDAGE

Threnody X

77.
The following day, the priest hurries
    To my father and solemnly swears
That there's been a misunderstanding;
    That his master had no intention
Of keeping the young newlyweds
    Under his thumb: "So what you need
To be now is all sweet and sugar,
    And just humor the old bugger!"

78.
And so my father is placated,
    But to the priest he then spells out
His terms: that if he is sincere
    "I'll be wanting him to declare
The fact, for words could not express
    My great anguish and deep distress.
Yet I'm prepared to show goodwill.
    I will swallow this bitter pill."

79.
He sends the priest back to his
    Master, who says: "All this senseless
Disagreement is futile indeed.
    We would do well to forget it!
Why would I make obligations
    That become broken promises?"
So all apologies are made,
    Marking an end to this brief feud.

They apologized to one another.

80.
All this takes place on the third day.
As for the groom, what can one say?
They keep pushing him towards me,
But he to this: "What for, tell me?"
On occasion, he looks me over,
Eyeing up my jewelry.
Whenever he opens his mouth,
Only gibberish dribbles out.

81.
All the guests enjoy dancing,
And this they do every evening.
Yet before the darkening night comes,
When everyone returns to their rooms,
Aesop is cajoled to declare *He asks for me.*
A husband's passionate desire
That husband and blushing wife should join.
We all listen to his oration.

82.
Few understand what is being said,
For he's either dumb or tongue-tied.
The old maid takes matters in hand,
And fills his ears with whispered prompts.
I must put up with this charade, *They took me to him.*
Accepting I am now married.
Ladies escort me to his chamber.
He appears in a coat of fur.

83.
He offers the ladies some sweets,
But they decline to take his treats,
So saying: "The time is surely nigh!"
But he responds: "Time's a plenty,
For the night couldn't be younger.
It's well short of the midnight hour."
Soon they have the measure of him,
And spirit me away with them.

84.
The guests who witnessed my doom
        Are beginning their journey home.
Aesop's father is still around,
        Although he too is homeward bound,
So saying: "Better for ye lovebirds
        If ye get onwards and upwards.
You shall stay here a few more days,
        After which you'll journey to my house."

85.
My father is also going hunting,
        So saying: "Have a horse waiting
For that fine son-in-law of mine!"
        To Aesop he declares the same.
The hands saddle him on the horse.
        They put his feet in the stirrups.
But he fears to whip the beast,
        Even though the horse is quite placid.

86.
They unleash the baying hounds,
        As a marching hare has been found.
Aesop looses his hound and follows,
But his horse is all ill at ease.
        My father must pull his horse up,
So crying: "The reins! Release your grip!"
        But Aesop lets go of the lot,
And would surely have met his death

He was lucky not to have broken his neck.

87.
Had hands not blocked this tearaway—
        For they'd already caught their prey.
He was shivering with mortal fear,
        Holding as he was the horse's ears,
Clutching its mane for all that's dear.
        Clattering hooves thrust high in the air,
Sending him flying from the saddle—
        But catch they did this flying missile.

88.
The party decides, then and there,
        That the less I know the better.
My father is ever more perturbed:
        He sees that Aesop is disturbed.
The son-in-law prattles and rambles.
        They suggest he practice silence.
For whenever anything is said,
        He shows that he's soft in the head.

MY FATHER'S GREAT REMORSE

Threnody XI

89.
Too soon will I be leaving behind
The beloved home of my childhood.
For it seems we are setting off
Long before I thought we would leave.
For Father must gather his men
And set off to war once again.
Not without tears do I recall
The sadness of that spectacle.

They prepare to depart.

90.
My father is so grief-stricken
At the prospect of my leaving,
He opts to keep me in the nest,
So saying: "Sure she hasn't flown yet!
If blame is to be handed out,
It means someone has caused it!
I am culpable in every sense.
I must try now to make amends."

My father is greatly disturbed; having seen the fool for what he is, he doesn't want to send me to him.

91.
But the argument was made,
And it was right to speak of it,
That "plans need to be thought through twice!
There will be a right time and place.
People's feelings are running high.
We must allow time to pass by.
You can't just pound your fists.
You must find justifiable grounds!"

The persuasions of my stepmother.

92.
My father is filled with remorse,
        And feels thwarted by such advice:
"I may just as well slit my wrists!"
        Adding: "It is more than hopeless.
She lies beyond her father's reach;
        I have placed my child with a wretch!"
And so we set out on our way,
        Arriving there the following day.

SAYING FAREWELL TO MY BELOVED FATHER

Threnody XII

93.
We're all sitting down to the feast,
Though we find that there are few guests,
Except for those who came with us.
The poor fare just defies the eyes!
Aesop is acting as he usually does:
Whatever he's given, he gorges.
Does he think he is being polite,
Drawing with a fork on his plate?

A farewell banquet.

94.
Little can I say of his ways,
For his behavior is always
Unchanging. Whenever they take
Him to task, he ignores the rebuke.
But with me there is some discourse:
He makes it clear that a carriage
Must be constructed from my tent,
And I'll get all the help I want.

The Castellan's son wished to make a carriage out of my tent.

95.
The term familiarity breeds contempt
Finds new meaning with "been Aesop'd."
I dread Father's pending departure;
The day is drawing ever closer.
When the day comes for us to part,
Words for his child flow from his heart.
My father gives me his blessing,
And begs God for His protection.

Sorrow at the departure of my father.

96.
He recalls all my tears and pleas:
He knows what this marriage entails.
Should I suffer any injury,
I am to send word straight away.
He leaves some of his people here:
Watchmen to be his eyes and ears.
If they see or suspect anything,
They will bring it to his attention.

97.
For the management of the house,
My father leaves a friend of his
Behind to be the orderly:
Tasked with running things properly.
His wife has also to keep watch
Over me to ensure that my health
Does not suffer and I keep strong.
He is stupid. She is too young.

He leaves Master Bieniecki and his wife in charge.

98.
Why can't I stop this tearful flow?
For the answer you need to know
Of the love between two friends,
Or the love felt for one's parents.
So immense is each salty drop,
That they would turn paper to pulp.
If only some spell could be cast
To make him a thing of the past!

99.
I walk alongside my father
For a mile, but go no further.
My heart would hold me on this track,
But he orders me to turn back.
So I return, filled with sadness.
The old man, on seeing me like this,
Tries to give me consolation
By offering words of affection.

Master Krakowski declares his affection for me.

100.
But looking for cheer is wasted effort,
    For where would I find such comfort?—
Cheer from Aesop's charm and grace?
    Comfort from his father's strictness:
Which he shows day in and day out
    When tyrannizing the household?
And with every word Aesop utters,
    My soul just shivers and shudders.

MY HATEFUL LIFE WITH AESOP

Threnody XIII

101.
Since he has most solemnly sworn
To surrender sole possession
Of the house and land, he departs,
Knowing his schemes have been thwarted.
Before leaving, he speaks with the friend,
He whom my father has left behind,
The one who is to run the house.
It's a speech with a stinging surprise:

Having promised to hand over the estate, he leaves behind his orderlies.

102.
"I'm going to be on my way now,
But on no account can I allow
Them to have free run of the place;
For I must protect my interests
And make sure that what's mine is safe.
God knows what they'll do to the place!
So I'm leaving my orderly behind,
And ye will all do his bidding!"

103.
And to this there comes the response:
"What's going on in that head of yours?
Is all this a practical jest?
Need I remind you of your pledge?
How do you expect me to work,
Pandering to a cock of the walk?
My master will know of your plan,
Cos' I'll not be taking the blame!"

He insulted Bieniecki.

104.
And here the old man is taken
By fury and loss of reason.
About to let loose with his fists,
Before he does so, he desists.
He sends messengers on ahead,
Almost opting to go instead,
With a note on this little spat,
Relating how he's been attacked.

He informs my father.

105.
My father was filled with sorrow
And anger prior to his journey.
But on hearing of this outrage,
He swears in the foulest language
That someone needs to pay a price.
But then a second runner rides
Up and says there is no urgency,
As the old man has snuck away.

My father was so angry that he wanted to go back at once, but just then a messenger on horseback came riding up and informed him that Master Krakowski had left—they only exchanged letters.

106.
So my father tries diplomacy
One more time, and sends a strongly
Worded letter, making it plain
That all parties have a bargain
To keep, and that it must be kept.
The old man writes, saying he's left,
But adds that my own happiness
Flies in the face of these complaints.

107.
Having achieved a victory
Of sorts, my father lays down the law:
Henceforth, we are to take guidance
From the orderlies left in charge.
So now there's just Aesop and I,
And with every day that goes by,
I can see him for the man he is,
For he has the run of the place.

Master Krakowski left, and his son remained with me.

108.
My heart is like an open wound
Bleeding from this piercing affront:
That the crown of my home is worn
By the most ignorant of men.
But here the crown's but a trinket,
And there is much bewilderment
Whenever vile King Aesop speaks
On history or politics.

109.
He stamps about, he rants and raves,
He delights in being obnoxious.
He wants women sent to the fires.
In all, seventy executioners
Are summoned to put them to death.
They had allowed rain wet his coat.
These women, he holds, are to blame—
They will know better the next time.

His orders.

When rain wet his gown, he ordered local ladies to be put to the fires for having let the rain in, he called for seventy executioners because he couldn't think of another number.

110.
And the church fares little better.
He wants to see it a burning pyre
After lice jumped from the rafters—
His scalp couldn't be itchier!
The priest must face the consequences—
There he is with his bell-ringers,
Combing nooks, crannies and pews,
Doing their best to sweep out the lice.

He also ordered the priest to be burnt with the church for having allowed lice into the church.

111.
Such were the orders that he gave,
All you could really do is laugh.
But mine is laughter mixed with tears;
For these are my blushing years,
Still filled with hope for a future.
And so I struggle with despair.
His talk is never going to help,
For that only brings troubled sleep.

112.
He really would talk to anyone,
Engaging peasants all day long
In discussions about their ploughs,
Their farms, and feed for the cows.
But all you need's a gust of wind
And he'll suddenly fall silent.
He'll take a seat, despite the guest,
And have someone else play the host.

Conversing with anybody.

113.
And when his tongue starts to run loose,
He relates stories about his spouse.
I often see him gulping down
Seventy brimming goblets of wine:
"Sure isn't she hale and hearty,
And doesn't she have subtlety."
He also likes to give me credit
For a recent drinking habit.

When his tongue was loose, he would say things about me, and that I drink.

114.
At times, he gives me my title.
More often, he just makes little
Of me: "If you're not of the gentry,
Then why should I call you 'Lady?'"
There's no sense in my protesting
As he directs his oaths to heaven,
Silencing speech with a great shout,
Or with a knife chasing me about.

Sometimes he says: "my little voivodess!"—on other occasions—"you're a peasant girl."

115.
However, when I do fall ill,
He worries over every detail,
Such as the wood for my coffin.
They're told to find some decent pine!
He thinks of my convalescence
By filling the house with noise.
If it's not him, it's his farmers
Who take relish in slamming doors.

He worries about the coffin.

116.
And then someone teasingly says
That soon he'll be looking on the face
Of a baby son or daughter.
Well one may have shouted "Murder!"
So badly does he take the news.
He does not think it could be lies.
He journeys to Wrocław for a crib,
Blind fury hastening his trip.

He wishes to send someone to Wrocław for a crib.

117.
The inner rage he was born with
Rises and sees him sorely vexed.
He cannot control his passion,
For he knows nothing of reason
And is bereft of good judgment.
His storm must rage until it's spent:
He harangues the entire household,
Crying that he'd be better off dead.

118.
How these rages leave him fixated
On the frailty of my throat.
And nothing would make him happier
Than to open my veins and pour
The flowing blood into his bathtub.
One day, I felt his choking grip,
But my maid leapt into the fray
And bravely beat the beast away.

He had almost killed himself with the effort of strangling me, when a maid pulled him off.

119.
How can I begin to describe
The heinous ways of that Aesop?
Hellish days could run to years,
And now my life's a veil of tears.
But I shall not abandon hope
Just yet, for surely I can cope
Until the day my father comes
And releases me of these bonds!

MY FATHER DIES

Threnody XIV

120.
Father writes from his encampment,
Telling me not to be disheartened:
"I am setting out this instant,
And soon I'll be where I'm destined."
But on the course of his journey
He falls ill with dysentery.
Stricken with emptying bowels,
He doubles over and collapses.

In the camp my father fell ill with fever and dysentery.

121.
He first orders his entourage
To turn back, but then he directs
Them to the home of his niece,
Who lives within marching distance.
But fortune interferes again,
And as if by predestination,
They come to where each dead husband
Of my stepmother had met his end.

He ordered them to bring him to Madame Silnicka to Stratyn: they lost their way and brought him to Podkamień, home of the Voivode of Rus, where all the husbands of my stepmother had died.

122.
He feels his end is soon to come,
And thinks of where fate has brought him:
"Here it seems I will breathe my last,
I'll die like them, the dye's been cast."
Though he tries to affect some cure,
The voivode could do little more.
This is not something you can mend:
The doctor only shakes his head.

Great were the efforts of the voivode.

123.
My father feels death's grip squeeze hard,
And he cries: "Death, just do your worst!
But I am dying in the knowledge
That I've placed my child in bondage!
She lives the life of a prisoner,
And when I'm gone, who will save her?"
He makes some last desperate plans,
And assigns me powerful guardians.

He was worried about me.

124.
My father was most concerned
To enter onto the testament
The name of him who'd wear a crown:
He, the most celebrated of men!
My dying father makes his final
Appeal to someone he can call
Family. He prays that this action
Will right a most terrible wrong.

He makes His Majesty the King my guardian.

125.
Happiness, teetering on the scales,
Has turned to unyielding sadness.
For every glimmering hope is
But a path to light strewn with glass.
Behold the fire-eyed maid, Bellona!
She has left me bereft once again.
She took from me my father!
Could there be anything harder.

He died in Podkamień.

THEY CONSPIRE TO CONCEAL MY FATHER'S DEATH FROM ME

Threnody XV

126.
They hear of my father's passing
But they choose to say nothing.
My heart is filled with unease,
Knowing what it is I cannot face.
Ghostly dreams leave me unsettled.
I'll admit it: I am rattled!
My father must be on his way…
He'll surely be here any day!

127.
As is customary in this house,
Father and son speak in whispers.
When servants tell me of his death,
That very moment I clutch my heart.
Almost my life, there and then.
But they are quick with their lying:
"Sure isn't he as strong as an ox,
And he riding here on his horse?"

They keep news of his death from me.

128.
The old man calls us to Lublin,
And sends for Father, summoning
Him to present himself before
The seat of arbitration and law.
He states that matters are in hand,
And have almost been concluded.
But what is needed at this stage
Is for Father to show his face.

Master Krakowski writes, telling us to travel to Lublin for a court case.

129.
So greater is the urgency
    For Father to make an appearance.
Oh, I pray that we find him there!
    Let me not be counting each hour:
But then, I would hear ill tidings.
    If only I had an eagle's wings,
I would have flown from the spot,
    Out-soaring every chasing dart.

130.
We speedily journey onwards,
    And not far from the rendezvous
We spend the night in Markuszów,
    Guests of the home of Firlej.
My host tells me we're kith and kin;
    That he is married to my cousin.
But fate has also done him wrong:
    It seems that he married too young.

In Markuszów, Master Firlej invited us to his castle.

131.
Before anything, he is warned
    That I should remain ignorant
Of my father's recent demise:
    And he plays along with the ruse.
So he kindly invites a ghost
    To the castle, doing his utmost
To dispel my palpable terror,
    Saying my father will soon be here.

132.
His was a most successful ploy,
    And he held me there one more day,
Promising me all sorts of treats,
    Not to mention a sumptuous feast.
Drinking to his heart's content,
    Aesop is pleased with this arrangement.
Later he is put in a carriage
    And taken to his night's lodgings.

The Castellan's son got drunk.

133.
We set out the following day,
        And some miles along the way,
We find the old man with his troupe,
        Awaiting his beloved Aesop.
Though all the men are gathered,
        They feel that I am best ignored.
The congress does not tarry long—
        All are hastening to Lublin.

We journeyed with Master Krakowski.

134.
My heart is filled with disquiet,
        Suspecting, but fearing to admit
That something awful has happened.
        They must think I am deaf and blind,
So poorly do they keep secrets.
        They could be shouting in the street:
"Don't be about with reddened eyes,
        And no offering her condolences!"

135.
And then someone carelessly lets
        Slip: "I'd hate to cause you upset,
But you'll find your aunt near here,
        Confined to her bed… at death's door.
Her husband fed her dainty treats
        And then waited for the symptoms.
She has been clinging on in vain."
        They'd told me she'd gone to Lublin!

They told me my aunt was in Lublin—her husband had poisoned her, and she was recovering.

136.
I prepare to rush to her bedside,
        To clasp a dying woman's hand.
Unable to ease her distress,
        I will beg her forgiveness.
I ask that the horses be harnessed,
        As I wish to depart in all haste.
But the old man to this: "My dear,
        You are not going anywhere."

I wanted to go to her but Master Krakowski would not allow it.

137.
And each and every person in that
Household does their best to prevent
Me from finding out. The old man
Had schooled them well in deception.
But the nature of heartbreak
Will always find its deathly mark.
Truth follows a determined path:
I was always going to find out!

138.
This is a house of conspiracies.
Huddled in nooks and crannies,
They debate over their next move,
But nothing at all presents itself.
Aesop is champing at the bit,
But soon finds himself muzzled.
They are fearful that I suspect.
Or worse! That I will guess the truth.

139.
And so, I am left in this limbo,
Not knowing the what or the why
Of anything. I yearn to see my aunt,
So that I can unburden my heart.
But the old man forbids my going.
I rightly ask for an explanation,
But the only answer he can find
Is: "I won't say, if you don't mind."

I lamented to Madame Bieniecka that they had forbidden me from visiting my aunt.

140.
But then Aesop blurts it all out:
"It's high time that we put an end
To this maddening business."
Death has caused your father's demise!
And I cry: "How can you be sure?
Is this another sharpened dagger
With which you choose to prod my skin!?"
"A truer word I've never spoken!"

I COME TO KNOW THE DEVASTATING TRUTH

141.
How can words describe that instant?
	It just cannot be imagined.
Can one ever express in words
	How grief can tear a heart to shreds?
Just where could I find compassion
	Or comfort at this or any time?
I realize that my father's demise
	Has left me a life of loneliness.

142.
My hearing's altogether muffled,
	My sight has me terribly troubled.
The white-haired one, the one whom I
	Mentioned earlier, utters a cry
When she sees me flaying in bed.
	Aesop looks extremely concerned,
But like a child at a pageant,
	He thinks this is great excitement.

I suffered a nervous collapse.

143.
He fancies himself as a nurse
	With an apothecary of cures.
But he then shouts out my bedroom
	Window: "How great is our alarm
At the state of our listless patient!"
	He ambles over to the bed
And screams right into my ear:
	"It's high time you perked up, my dear!"

144.
My father's orderly finds out
	About the latest episode.
Like a man on a sacred mission
	He hastens to find the old man.
Struggling and gasping for air,
	He spews out the sorry story,
Only to behold a father's rage:
	How jaws tighten and eyes bulge.

Master Bieniecki met Master Krakowski by chance and informed him.

145.
The old man comes carrying a cane—
    A father is looking for his son.
Blind with fury, he shouts and roars.
    Stricken with fear, Aesop cowers
Behind the bed… was it under?
    But what bed has offered shelter
From a man so determined
    To mete out deserved punishment?

When Master Krakowski arrived, he beat his son with a stick.

146.
He thrashes Aesop with his cane,
    Leaving him stripe-cut to the bone.
The old man then seeks me out,
    Sending his man into the night
To find his wife and bring her thither—
    For at the time she was not there.
He feels I need consolation:
    His wife will play my kith and kin.

147.
He himself mustered the courage
    To deliver the following speech:
"Dear child, we all must reconcile
    Our lives to what is God's will.
You must accept that what happens
    Lies in the greater scheme of things.
In my heart you are my daughter,
    So please treat me as your father."

Master Krakowski speaks to me.

148.
He compounds my indignation
    When he confesses to having seen
In me a pleasing recompense
    For his son's inadequacies.
My answer is shrill and strident:
    "This life of mine is abhorrent!"
Deliver me, Death, from this fate,
    If you've but a crumb of comfort!

Even greater sorrow because of this.

149.
How can I express my sorrow,
    When it's beyond me to do so?
Lord, you have seen what they did.
    You have seen them crush my spirit.
Not only have I no consolation,
    But now I have no protection.
I contend with life as it stands,
    With Aesop as my life-long sentence.

Threnody XVI

150.
I inherited my father's estate,
But this is land for widowhood.
My stepmother hatches plans,
Stashing away my belongings.
And so the old man sends letters
And envoys to my stepmother.
Both parties prepare to contest
In court that which is my bequest.

Master Krakowski sent for the property to be taken over: my stepmother and I acquired legal ownership.

151.
Gradually people find out
That I know of my father's death.
They provide me with their accounts
And offer me their condolences.
As for our counter-petition,
The judge makes a just decision.
Sometimes effort is well spent:
I now own my father's estate.

The court reached its decision.

152.
And so we journey once again,
Returning to where it all began,
When so many tears were shed,
The day I became Aesop's bride.
And now all my sorrows and trials
Converge and rise to the surface.
Oh, to describe the emotion
As we approach my father's home!

We journeyed to Maciejowice.

153.
The trashing has left him unhinged
And has pushed him over an edge.
But Aesop is no soul in pain:
Bereavement is just too much fun.
He begins to gush and blather
About my beloved father.
He speaks of schemes that they had hatched
To keep me ignorant of his death.

The Castellan's son worries that someone will tell me of the death of my father, fearing that he will be beaten again.

154.
"Now I have something more to add:
Your beloved father is not dead.
It has all been a big mistake,
And you're just being melancholic.
If I had been in on the plot,
I would have soon set you straight.
He's in the land of the living,
And will be here any day now."

He kept the truth from me even though we wore mourning dress and were living on the estate.

I TRY TO TAKE AESOP IN HAND

Threnody XVII

155.
The old man says that he will leave:
        "So ye can get on with your life."
He takes the return road home,
        To return from whence he came.
But just as the dying show courage,
        So, too, must I try and manage
As best I can to make things right,
        Even when Aesop opens his mouth.

Master Krakowski departs from Maciejowice.

156.
He fancies that he can converse
        With men who spin fanciful phrases.
But they're all just a babbling host,
        Who love to yap, and love to boast.
Those who were once faithful and loyal
        Are now at Aesop's beck and call.
They can at least stop him spouting
        Twaddle on his every outing.

I employ educated servants, discerning that the Castellan's son will be more malleable when he isn't jabbering away to any old person.

157.
And I make my instructions clear:
        They must make every endeavor
To keep the deviant contained.
        At least here we're in agreement!
What's more, I repeat the adage:
        "The blacksmith shall never forge
What Mother Nature withholds."
        They see the truth in what I've said.

But in vain.

158.
He should know more of my bequest
And of its accompanying benefits.
We broach this difficult topic,
And indeed all he does is balk.
We urge him to ask the Hetmans
To grant him my family's standards.
"If you are forthright and sincere,
They'll surely bestow the honor."

They urge him to take the standards.

159.
The deviant keeps us on our toes
With a litany of queries.
"Tell me what you know of the cloth.
Of what is it made?" We grit our teeth
And patiently say: "Your asking
Means that you either know nothing
Or that you're feigning ignorance!
Well, we'll give you no such excuse.

He asks about the standards.

160.
It is smooth and velveteen,
And although it has clearly seen
Better days, it has inspired
Many a chivalrous exploit,
Not to mention a fine soldier.
This is its plume of soft feather.
The armor stands by the mattress—
Its glint is what every Turk fears."

161.
He listens, but has his own ideas—
Wanting to add accessories.
Fancying himself a man of fashion,
He wants it to be crimson.
He imagines velvet and tails
Hemmed with the fur of dormice.
"It could be a cozy blanket,
Keeping me warm of a cold night."

He wants for the standard to be velvet, hemmed with dormouse fur and surrounded with tails.

162.
They try to stop him there and then.
They try to make him see reason.
They remind him of principles
And the increase to his prestige.
But he's not to be prevailed upon,
And reveals his trepidation:
"I know ye would all celebrate,
If I were killed on the battlefield?"

He is fearful of meeting his death.

163.
And again, we try persuasion:
"Think of the triumphs of brave men
Committed to the noble cause.
They've never known a day's sickness.
But should the fates ever decide
That ye are to die a soldier's death,
Think about your heroic legacy;
The tales people will tell of ye.

164.
Dying bravely with a knowing smile,
God will send a caring angel,
Who will take your spirit to heaven.
And great will be the procession
As a crown is placed on your head."
And Aesop to this: "My father
Will be there and holding a cane,
And he will thrash me for all time."

He says his father will beat him in the next world.

165.
Unable to make any progress,
They come to tell me the bad news,
So saying: "He cares not one jot.
That is the unfortunate truth."
It was not just wasted effort,
But now he is more difficult.
At the end of all my tethers,
I'm in bed on doctor's orders.

I AM TOO ILL TO TRAVEL TO MY FATHER'S FUNERAL

Threnody XVIII

166.
Ashes to ashes, dust to dust,
With these words we are laid to rest—
Often spoken in a tired voice.
His grieving wife then arrives
And speaks of the funeral.
As a family we shall all
Administer a sacrament
That should not be administered.

My stepmother informs me of my father's funeral.

167.
Oh, what bitterness poisons
The sweetness of my memories!
And I shudder at the very thought
That not so long ago, he sat
Amongst his soldiers and broke
Bread with them by way of thanks
For their commitment and toil.
Now he is lying in the soil.

The funeral is in Lwów, where he had been a commissar for a year.

168.
What an unacceptable prize
For years of courageous service!
How many years did he deserve
To be given? Surely a life
Which abandons all honors
Is deserving of more kindness.
For when the battle lines are lost,
We pray to men of courage

169.
To deliver the heroic goods.
        And though my heart knows only loss,
Duty asserts itself in law
        And I prepare for the journey.
But my health is terribly frail,
        And that night I fall gravely ill.
Gripped by fever and delirious,
        How I survived is anyone's guess.

I fell ill in the night.

170.
Unable to get out of bed,
        My body feels lifeless and tired.
Full of false concern, the old man
        Requests of me that I remain,
Lest I make myself much worse.
        Even though I am barely conscious,
This so clearly smacks of bad taste,
        That I should just die for sheer spite!

Master Krakowski also sent a messenger, asking me not to travel.

171.
Even though the time is pressing,
        I find myself still bedridden,
Having not regained my vitality
        As promptly as it had left me.
I've sent my people upon their way,
        And now the patient shall prepare
To partake of a round of laments,
        Commending a soul into God's hands.

THE FIRST CHINK OF LIGHT

Threnody XIX

172.
And then there comes to my ears
Rumors that things are moving apace,
That my family is taking steps
To get me away from Aesop.
Sensing that something is afoot,
The old man summons the one-eyed
Priest. The two conspire and hatch
A plot of devious subterfuge.

It was heard that one of my relations had said that I wish to divorce the Castellan's son.

173.
He is to be alert and obliging,
And to tend to my every whim.
In particular, he is to gauge
My happiness in this marriage.
The report is to be honest,
So that the old man will know best
How to plot a happier future
For his son and daughter-in-law.

So Master Krakowski sends the priest to me for a heart-to-heart.

174.
The priest is certainly a clever sort.
You could say, a master of his art.
He chooses to be sympathetic
And attempts some light chit-chat,
Mingled with probing questions.
He tries to win my confidence
By saying: "I so greatly regret
That I joined you to a half-wit.

The priest looks to gauge my state of mind.

175.
You are not in the least to blame.
Your own father must have done some
Soul-searching. The time is now right
To give some thought to your own plight.
Allow me to guide you in this,
I am speaking from experience.
You must rid yourself of this fool,
To release the cur, leash and all."

176.
His holiness can try and try!
I know exactly what he's up to.
He wants to hear all the gossip
About my life with his Aesop.
However, his is wasted effort.
I've done the rounds with his sort.
There will be no meeting of minds.
I say to him: "You've been splendid.

I gave nothing away—I knew his tricks and games.

177.
But I have not the slightest idea
Where all this could be leading.
I am content enough with fortune.
I accept all that's been given
Until the sweet release of death:
I care not for any other path.
Heaven is the ultimate promise.
We must all carry our crosses."

178.
He knows that he has met his match,
And he even admits as much.
"I wish only to know you better.
But now I can say with candor
That it never entered my head
That you would at all contemplate
Revealing this unpleasantness.
I greatly admire your forbearance."

He admitted that he had wished to know my mind.

179.
I have thrown them off the scent,
        With them thinking I am content.
They have no idea that I plan
        To flee both them and this prison.
But if my heart could only act,
        I would run from here just as fast
As my two legs could carry me.
        I'd be long gone before they knew.

Their minds had been put at ease.

MY FAMILY COMES TO MY AID

Threnody XX

180.
God looks down from heaven
    And sees that he must intervene
To hearten my flagging spirit—
    For it has given up the ghost.
But my father's spirit inspires
    My family, who are of one voice.
They know that they must all act
    Now, if I am to be rescued.

181.
And he of whom I have spoken,
    Now sitting proudly on his throne,
Whose head and crown would be one,
    Agrees to see a poor woman.
I speak of my wretchedness,
    And leave him with few doubts
That I will take every step
    Needed to rid myself of Aesop.

His Highness the King, then commander of the army, met with me.

182.
He offers me kingly advice,
    And presents the alternatives.
But before I take any steps,
    He advises that I mend bridges
With my stepmother. She can negotiate
    My freedom. But it's all her fault!
She who placed me in this bondage
    Is both felon and crown witness!

He wishes for me to make peace with my stepmother so that she may serve my interests.

183.
When the throne is vacated
By one who is better suited
To life as an abbot, father
And son journey to Warsaw.
They join other powerful men
On this important occasion
To cast votes in an election
By which a new king is chosen.

Following the abdication of King Kazimierz, an election was held.

184.
Senators, envoys and ambassadors,
And those you could call homebirds,
Undertake this important trip.
The old man in the name of Aesop
Will cast the family ballot.
And just like all those assembled,
He knows that the choice of ruler
Could strongly affect his future.

Master Krakowski orders his son to travel to Warsaw.

185.
He orders me to remain at home,
Saying: "You've only yourself to blame
For having dismissed your own court,
Being so concerned for their comfort.
Well, they're now about their business.
You thought there'd be no harm in this,
That you'd be all fine and dandy,
But now you have troubles aplenty."

He was angry at me for having engaged a retinue of servants.

I ENTER THE SANCTUARY OF THE CONVENT

Threnody XXI

186.
Even though I have been busied
With packing chests and what-not,
It is not without exultation
That I boldly tell the old man
About the protector and his nod
To me on bridging the divide
With my stepmother. Mending a fence
Is but the first roll of our dice.

I tell Master Krakowski that His Majesty the Hetman wishes for us to make peace with my stepmother, today he is the king.

187.
With great reluctance, the old man
Agrees to my accompanying
Them. But that is all he'll concede!
For then he becomes preoccupied
With ensuring that I'm kept isolated,
So that no one pays me a visit.
All holy smiles, he begs the nuns
To provide me with warm lodgings.

He orders me to undertake the journey and for me to reside in a convent.

188.
Heaven must have guided his mind
And clouded his better judgment.
For now I have the breathing space
To follow through with my plans.
I set out with a spring in my step
And travel directly to the convent.
I am granted entry to a place
Which is my holy of holies.

I arrived.

189.
Aesop is perplexed and speechless
At these mystifying arrangements.
He simply cannot understand why
I'm being housed in a nunnery.
Anger is written on his face,
And it soon rises to the surface
With a scene made greatly worse
By the fact that he's in his cups.

The Castellan's son berates me for staying in the convent.

190.
He completely loses the run
Of himself: "So is it a nun
You want to be!? Do you really
Think that I'll be so easily
Fooled!? Those nuns would do better
If they stuck to the rosary.
I have a mind to raze the convent
And drag you over the scorched ground!"

191.
Carrying the very same surname,
But having earned a fearsome
Reputation for his skill with a sword,
Aesop's brother-in-law tries hard
To allay all fears and creeping doubts.
But all his efforts are wasted:
"How can I make him see reason
When he doesn't want to listen?"

The Sword-Bearer of the Crown restrains him.

192.
He pulls him away from the grate,
But Aesop's fingers are clasped tight.
The brother-in-law tries reason,
And threatens to tell the old man
Everything. But threats prove futile.
He hurls at me every kind of foul
And derogatory language.
He then makes a violent lunge.

193.
Had it not been for the blessed grate,
He would have grabbed me by the throat.
They drag him forcibly away,
His mouth foaming from the frenzy.
I'm left desperately shaken,
My heart all pounding and broken.
By the hour my sight is worsening.
My eyes must be tired of seeing.

He would have beaten me had it not been for the grate.

194.
I could find myself out on a limb
If I were ever to become infirm.
It simply bears no thinking about.
I'd be left for dead on damp wood!
I have no claim to house or lands.
We are a couple living on handouts!
The old man has title to the lot.
Between them they have me buried!

Having cried my fill of tears, I consider my position.

195.
Can a person be so contented?
Can words so readily placate?
The city of honor is shocked
To hear of my desperate act.
But it is now time to take the bull
By the horns and show an iron will:
To strike out for a life thought lost.
May God be merciful and just!

Threnody XXII

196.
I am visited by relatives
And receive supportive letters.
And one day, she who wears a miter
Upon her head, comes to visit.
I am so pleased and gratified,
My darkened world floods with light.
For these are people who govern
With steely determination!

Princess Radziwiłłowa comes to see me.

197.
Oh, how nature has bestowed upon
Them such virtues of condescension,
That they can be so generous
To me in my hour of crisis!
They declare their heartfelt concern,
And say that they will champion
My cause. They've made a commitment
And have the bit between their teeth.

198.
Their advice is to hold the course
And to keep my strength and courage.
I am to remain in my sanctuary
And enjoy the hospitality.
"Though it has not been brought to light,
The world will soon know of your plight.
Esteemed minds have a strategy
To free you from your bondage."

She discusses the possibility of divorce with me.

199.
For the moment I am to box clever,
And remain within the sanctuary
Of the convent. And on no account
Should I even think of going back
To the old man. Aesop's heinous
Behavior is my best excuse:
His tirade and violence has upset
Me so much that I must stay in bed.

The strategy—to remain in the convent.

200.
Well the gloomy truth is that my
Health has taken an almighty
Beating. But I am determined
To one day enjoy health and strength.
And so, I call for the physician,
Who doles out doctorly wisdom.
I begin a cure of medicines,
Which only brings me uneasy dreams.

I take medicines.

201.
The old man is wondering aloud
Why I've not returned to the fold.
Wanting to dispel all suspicion,
I send him word of my condition.
You could say he was suspicious:
Many would say incredulous.
He summons the doctor and asks
Him to explain his diagnosis.

He had a doctor come and see me.

202.
It is not the diagnosis
He wished to hear, so he decides
To visit the stricken patient.
My symptoms have just worsened!
And yet, he must have gone to some
Bother, as this was a heady time,
For there was great commotion
Prior to the coronation.

Master Krakowski himself paid me a visit.

I MAKE PEACE WITH MY STEPMOTHER

Threnody XXIII

203.
He has been happily chosen
    To rule our glorious kingdom;
And yet no one had ever fancied
    Him as a serious candidate.
On the day that he was crowned,
    His star was in the ascendant.
And though the heavens were smiling,
    This would be a short honeymoon.

The election of King Michał.

204.
The clouds are beginning to lift,
    As my guardians are firmly fixed
On achieving a felicitous
    End for their damsel in distress.
And I am comforted to know
    That a man of such high stature
Has declared himself my champion
    And guaranteed my protection.

Our present king advises me to come to an accord with my stepmother.

205.
He insists that I build closer
    Relations with my stepmother,
As we cannot allow a dispute
    Or some unresolved family feud
To distract us from our efforts.
    Sure aren't we now allies of sorts?
I will gladly bury the hatchet!
    It's all water under the bridge.

206.
The representatives of both
Sides gather on an agreed date.
The atmosphere is cordial.
All endeavor to be affable.
Grievances are plainly stated.
Solutions are negotiated.
Efforts most worthy of applause,
Were we both not at loggerheads.

Peace is made with my stepmother.

207.
I'm fighting a losing battle,
Teetering over a barrel.
I try to be diplomatic,
She, in turn, wants everything back.
I try to parry and retreat,
But it seems nothing is sacred.
She negotiates for pleasure:
What was mine… now belongs to her!

The accord was strong, but there was little alternative.

208.
My advisors are left aghast
And agog at what they've witnessed.
The old man has them here to advise
Me in these negotiations,
But they never expected their charge
To yield so much ground with such ease.
They confer and conclude: "Perhaps
There is method in her madness!?"

209.
I try and explain my reasons,
Searching my mind for justifications:
"Why should I be belligerent
When generosity's in my gift?
Our lives are so closely entwined,
I'll scratch no more this open wound.
I will not be discourteous toward
Her, whom I hold in high regard."

210.
The old man is bothered by no such
Twinges of conscience. He hatches
Schemes. His festering resentment
At seeing me there in the convent
Has him plotting desperate acts.
He is determined at all costs
To snatch me from under their nose
And restore me to my rightful place.

Master Krakowski senses that divorce is the next step.

211.
But I am forewarned of this plot
By him whom I have alluded
To, although I sincerely doubt
Whether he actually cares a jot.
Honesty is always the best
Policy for feathering your nest:
He thinks that playing politics
Is a great way of getting rich.

The Sword-Bearer of the Crown warns me to proceed with care.

212.
But I don't need convincing,
As I can see a knot of men
Through the window of my cell.
These are my slinking sentinels:
His band of brigands and villains.
They're watchful and ready to pounce.
Should I ever put my toe outside,
They'll bundle me into sackcloth.

He orders my abduction.

213.
But when the plot comes to nothing,
Master Krakowski sends his son:
"Take the carriage, and fetch your wife!
It's time you established your rights.
And if the stepmother sets terms,
You should comply with all her whims.
Once you have her in the carriage,
Drive the horses home at a charge!"

Master Krakowski orders his son to spirit me away from the convent.

214.
He should've looked before he leaped.
    Aesop knows he's out of his depth.
My guardian stands bold and true,
    And says: "She is not going with you!"
O great monarch! O beam of light!
    O man of majesty and strength!
How could the fool ever face down
    Him who was Marshal and Hetman!?

215.
My guardian stands by my side
    As Aesop's party beg and plead.
They ask, why all the unpleasantness,
    When I have the best of husbands?
"Sure hasn't he devoted his life
    To honoring his beloved wife?"
But my stepmother has her plan,
    And readily puts her foot down.

His Majesty the King stood by me like a guardian.

216.
Tonight there is a gathering
    To celebrate our deception.
The men strategize and extol.
    One lady pampers and consoles.
Both my father and her husband
    Had shared an unshakable bond.
Now I can see with my own eyes
    The extent of her influence.

The Lady Voivode of Kraków, who today is a nun.

I DECLARE MY INTENTIONS

Threnody XXIV

217.
Although it is right to celebrate,
We are not out of the woods yet.
They would rest on their laurels,
But I leave nothing to chance.
I fill the silence with a shrill:
"Let's end this now, once and for all!
I only contemplate divorce,
And will inform Aesop of this."

I declare my intention to seek a divorce.

218.
My guardian delivers the news
To the old man in person, whose
Countenance is one of disbelief.
His charge no longer wishes to live
With Aesop. "But this business
Shouldn't involve unpleasantness.
We can settle it in such a way
That the world need never know."

219.
But the old man is adamant:
"I'll hear this from the horse's mouth!"
He comes with a heartwarming smile,
And proceeds to wax lyrical:
"My dear, a disturbing report
Has reached my ears, leaving me hurt
And upset. So tell me now, please,
That what they're saying is nonsense."

Master Krakowski tries to reason with me.

220.
His voice is assured but his eyes,
Reveal ten panic-filled stories.
Having seen so many outrages,
I am steeled to what he'll say next:
"You are surely acting on a whim
That will ultimately bring harm
To yourself. Do not choose a road
That you must know is a dead end."

221.
Why should I be meek and pleasant
When I have no wish to be silent?
I've held my tongue for far too long,
And will indulge him no longer:
"Are you really insinuating
That this is some flight of fancy?
My family are not in the business
Of peddling salacious lies!

I am resolved on my course of action.

222.
I have told them my sorry tale.
They've heard every sordid detail.
It's the story of an innocent
Made the wife of a deviant!
My father regretted his part
And suffered a broken heart.
He knew only too well of my fate,
Trapped in a house of ill repute.

223.
Had he not so tragically died,
He would surely have rescued
Me. But it wasn't to be, and so
I was left to suffer in silence.
Now the shoe's on the other foot,
And I will bring this episode
To an end. Your threats I ignore!
I strike for freedom and honor!"

AESOP BEGS ME TO RECONSIDER

Threnody XXV

224.
I will not stop with heated words.
This is a time for valiant deeds.
We begin annulment proceedings
By writing detailed petitions
To the Papal Nuncio, our argument
Being that Aesop is incompetent.
My father must also shoulder blame:
We are forced to besmirch his name.

I sue for a divorce.

225.
And then the old man sends his son,
Warned not to come back on his own:
"Do whatever you can to salvage
The wreckage of your marriage.
Get down on your bended knees
Before her and beg forgiveness.
Plead with your wife to desist!
Sing her serenades if you must!"

Master Krakowski sends his son to beg my forgiveness.

226.
He comes to me all contrite
And repeats what he has been told.
His eyes tell a different story:
"What can I say, I'm so sorry!
If you follow through with this plan,
I'll be made a slave once again
Of my father's grim tyranny.
You wouldn't ever want that, would you?

227.
Don't leave me, my sweet Anusiu!"
    And I to this: "My Kazusiu!
I wish it could be otherwise,
    But I'll be having this divorce!
Do not give me those hang-dog eyes,
    For you and the entire world knows
That I was kind and you were not.
    I leave you to the care of God.

I give him my answer.

228.
How can there be a marriage
    When the bride is but a hostage?
Dragged up the aisle by force;
    Given no choice but to say yes.
But I will forgive all the hurt
    And will even go so far as to
Wish you all health and happiness.
    I will rejoice in all your joys."

THE OLD MAN CORRUPTS PROCEEDINGS AND I HAVE SUITORS

Threnody XXVI

229.
When he sees I'm not for turning,
The old man plumbs for bribery.
He promises me heaven and earth,
All things of monetary worth.
He's so certain he'll dazzle me
With the return of my property:
Every blade of grass and trinket,
And anything else I may add.

Master Krakowski visits and promises to restore to me all my property.

230.
O snake, hiding in the long grass!
You will never lure or seduce
Prey with greed and hypocrisy.
For that you need other colors.
This time I am taking no risks.
Not like she who lost paradise.
For the fruit of unknown wisdom
Is not worth the loss of freedom.

231.
He knows that I cannot be bought,
That we must stand before a court
In order to settle this impasse.
The Papal Nuncio sends us
To an officiating judge,
Whose task is to hear all complaints.
He is to reconcile us both,
Or failing that, make a judgment.

The legate sends us to the judge.

232.
But the judge is no peacemaker,
Nor is he an honest broker,
Having taken the evil coin
To shilly-shally and bog down
The proceedings indefinitely.
He is rubbing his hands with glee.
He makes his justification,
Spouting some spurious reason.

The judge accommodates the other side.

233.
My protector gets word of these
Most devious shenanigans.
He arranges to see the judge,
Against whom he levels charges:
"Perhaps you would explain to me
The reason for this strange delay?
Is it that you feel deliberations
Will come easier in my absence?

His Majesty the King goes to see the judge.

234.
I'll have ye know one simple truth:
That I take a dim view of corrupt
Officials. And so here I'll stay,
And keep you under my watchful gaze.
You must know you're playing with fire,
That such games will get you nowhere.
You are a judge, so adjudicate!
Or a sorry price will be paid."

235.
Now wise to their every trick,
The just response is like with like.
The king confides in those he trusts,
Looking to the one he trusts most
To be my very eyes and ears.
He keeps me abreast of our progress
And acts in the name of the king.
His presence, a watchful warning.

To help serve my interests, he assigns me his cousin, Master Koniecpolski, who has some knowledge of such transactions.

236.
Out of the blue, the pious nuns
Become perturbed by my presence.
It's a sea-change like no other,
But they fear their benefactor
May withdraw his benevolence.
His benefaction means so much,
If he dragged me out of the gate,
They would hardly bat an eyelid.

The nuns were greatly worried and wanted to send me from the convent.

237.
The Papal Nuncio soon hears word
Of this most shameful episode.
He sends the nuns a stinging letter,
Ordering them to reconsider
Such an unconscionable action.
The Nuncio then tells the old man
To reassure the fretful abbess
That he will still fill their coffers.

The Nuncio takes the nuns to task.

238.
As long as the court case continues,
My future hangs in the balance.
Here I remain stuck in storage,
Far too scared to venture forth.
But I am kept abreast of events,
The cut and thrust of exchanges,
By a steady flow of visitors,
Who gabble out worthless advice.

239.
My guests are of all varieties,
Including a clutch of suitors,
Who'd be happy to stay all day
And sing sweet nothings in my ear.
Sweetness is all fine and dandy,
But my life is each fretful day:
The court may find in their favor,
Leaving me stuck here forever!

Different suitors express their admiration.

240.

They put the horse before the cart
  As they fawn and congratulate
Me on an outcome that is far
  From settled. I admire their air
Of optimism, but when they declare
  Their undying loyalty, and swear
They'll save me from Aesop's clutches,
  I'd like to pat them on their heads.

They serve me in the divorce.

THE COURT FINDS IN MY FAVOR BUT CALLS FOR AN INQUISITION

Threnody XXVII

241.
Friends offer me kindnesses;
The old man makes obnoxious threats.
But bluster is all that's left to him
As my moment has finally come.
The city has found in my favor:
I am Aesop's wife no longer.
"You can't drag a girl up the aisle,
And marry her against her will."

The judge became angry at Master Krakowski, who had threatened him.

242.
The judgment also stipulates
That I present twelve witnesses,
Who can relate in their own words
How I was placed in this bondage;
Who saw events with their own eyes,
And who heard my desperate cries.
Twelve seems like a small number
When I could call a small army.

A decree is made, and an inquisition ordered.

243.
We thank the court for its ruling
And look to form an inquisition,
With witnesses principally plucked
From the obeisance of servants
Who heard and saw the coercions:
How my father showed no conscience.
The white-haired ones seize the moment,
And provide a vivid account.

I form my inquisition.

244.
My stepmother, who knows the most
    About my sad and sorry past,
Paints a grim picture for the court,
    Saying it was all my father's fault.
Today I call you my Mother,
    Because you have earned this gesture!
You spoke of unsavory doings,
    Throwing your good name to the winds.

My stepmother testifies at my inquisition.

245.
A leopard doesn't change its spots,
    So say mean-spirited skeptics,
Who will not be budged from the
    Thought of there being some agenda
Which she's kept hidden from view.
    But I understand her candor:
She's holding true to her promise
    To undo these terrible wrongs.

Opinions about her are divided.

246.
She lays the whole episode bare,
    Every sordid detail and more.
She even says she argued against
    This most ill-considered match.
The picture becomes all too clear.
    It is a most troubling story:
A girl had a callous father,
    Who gave her away like barter.

247.
The old man doesn't take this lying down
    And provides a different version.
He parades a pity of strangers,
    Whom he has pressed into service.
They spin a cock-and-bull story
    With alarming alacrity.
But the judge isn't that stupid:
    He chews up fibbers for breakfast.

The other side presents their inquisition.

I AM GRANTED A DIVORCE
BUT I MUST RETURN EVERYTHING

Threnody XXVIII

248.
I win the battle but not the war.
The judge has a surprise in store.
I must return every last gift
With an inventoried list.
Not only do I have to return
Aesop's gifts, but every wedding
Present given by the guests.
On this point, the judge will not budge.

I am ordered to give back everything.

249.
I hand back the pretty necklace,
The one with sparkling diamonds
And sumptuous sapphire rubies—
A visual feast for ladies' eyes.
And so I'm truly despondent,
As I had always intended
To hold on to it if I could.
But they were having none of it.

250.
There is another stumbling block.
Never thinking they'd want it back,
I'd made a quiet reconnaissance
Of the latest jewelry designs,
And then had the necklace altered.
And now I'm exasperated,
Justifying this action to men
Who have no clue about fashion.

I had refashioned an old brooch, which he had given me, and great was the kerfuffle and loud were the demands for me to give it back in its original condition.

251.
The goldsmith only shakes his head,
And says it cannot be restored:
"I would have to melt it down
And refashion it once again."
He explains the entire process
With enthusiasm and competence.
But I know nothing of antiques,
And this is of a bygone age.

252.
With some degree of reluctance,
They agree to take back the necklace.
But having counted each and every stone,
They find that some are missing.
I'm the guilty party, of course,
And now they indulge in malice.
The goldsmith must state under oath
Just how much the necklace is worth.

253.
The brave jeweller shows no fear,
And says what they don't want to hear:
"It wasn't worth much in the first place,
Sure weren't the stones very loose
And the workmanship very poor.
It's worth a few coins, but no more.
And if the truth be really told,
You'd get more for the melted gold."

254.
The old man's ears are burning red,
With eyes fixed on the poor goldsmith.
He grabs his bone-smashing stick,
And raises it, about to strike:
"How dare you insult me so!
That is a brooch of great value!"
He would have beaten him to death
Had the king's man not intervened.

He wanted to beat the goldsmith, but was stopped by the servant of King Michał, who had been sent by the king to request that he not quarrel with me.

255.
I scour every trunk and drawer,
Down to the last cup and saucer.
They can take every last piece,
Just as long they leave me in peace.
My stepmother is also asked
To return a silver-framed portrait
Of the old man's ancestors:
Each one as ugly as the next!

I give back all the gifts.

256.
They're like a tidings of magpies,
Wanting every stitch of clothes,
Every last piece of furniture,
And all my jewels and finery.
If we don't produce every item,
We'll never see the back of them.
What should be thrown onto the fire
Is listed and bundled with care.

I give him back his things.

257.
When the time comes to convey
These goods to the arbitrator,
Uppity maids with beady eyes
Look them over for any signs
Of damage, scratches, or wear and tear.
And lo and behold, there is uproar
When they cannot find a dress, saying:
"Ye'll deliver it here, anon!"

Gowns from childhood, which he had kept.

258.
They are fixedly determined
To take back every last trinket,
And to leave me with nothing.
I even add things that are mine,
Or at least what I thought I'd owned,
But it seems that all is forfeit
To a band of circling vultures,
Marking time over a stricken corpse.

259.
They continue to tick off items
        And make sure there's no damage.
But silence descends on the room
        When we hand over a child's gown.
It is basically a soiled pat
        Which they just dumped in a basket.
And then there are moth-eaten garments
        Which must have made the poor moths retch.

They order me to account for all of his possessions.

260.
I do not forget his musket,
        Which he says he has always kept
For the defense of home and hearth.
        He is obviously a crack shot
As he's kept foes at arms-length—
        Sometimes boastful talk spares the deed!
This weapon, he brags, has history—
        German craftsmanship gone rusty!

261.
I have had my fill of this list,
        Looking now for a pistolet
Which may have never existed.
        But I make up the deficit
And purchase a brand new firearm—
        It's not the first such occasion!
Nothing is worth the trouble they cause,
        I'm long past the point of outrage.

Great was the kerfuffle when I did not hand back a small pistol, and it was only settled when I gave him another in its place.

262.
But for all my acquiescence,
        I had hoped to keep the carriage:
So gleaming, stately and grandiose,
        If not a little worn from use.
Many have praised the upholstery,
        Which is a brighter shade of white-blue.
The seats have a velvet softness,
        Even though they've lost their studs.

Carriage.

263.
The coach gleams brightly from afar.
Its panels almost hold the air,
Being so exquisitely gilded.
The hood is a fine piece of wood,
Although it has more holes than cheese.
Whenever there are heavy rains,
We hold blankets above our heads
And pass the time counting droplets.

264.
The horses have a noble gait.
Their heads are high, each leg is straight.
Because they are such handsome beasts,
Aesop often made gushing boasts:
"I'd prefer a coat made of tarant
Over lynx any day, wouldn't
You? If I have one or two skinned,
I'll happily give you the hind."

He possessed tarant horses, and he boasted that he would have them skinned and a robe made from the pelts, and that he would give me any cast-offs.

265.
So I've given every last stitch,
And now I have nothing left.
But my conscience is clear:
I couldn't have given more.
He releases me of my oath,
But is not finished with me yet.
He draws up a list in his head
Of imaginary things he's owed.

He released me from my oath, but quarreled with me as of old.

A NEW PROPOSAL OF MARRIAGE AND BITTERSWEET FREEDOM

Threnody XXIX

266.
Finally it has been decreed:
This marriage is now null and void.
The court reads aloud its judgment:
"There is not a shadow of doubt
That this was marriage most foul.
What transpired was truly shameful."
The decree separates man and slave,
Ending in law this hideous life.

The final decree.

267.
Or so I'd every right to presume!
But they make an appeal to Rome,
Couching the wording of their plaint
As if I had caused the affront.
And while he has me in his sights,
I remain a guest of the nuns.
I know the fox is lying in wait,
Hoping that I'll venture outside.

The other side appeals to Rome.

268.
Suitors lavish praise and are courteous,
Treating me like the person I once
Was. But these are empty gestures,
For I'm still a guest with the nuns.
I do not wish to offend anyone
By pooh-poohing the coronation
Or the national euphoria,
But not everyone's whooping for joy.

They make their bows as of old, but I fob them off, telling them that they'll have their answer on the day of the king's coronation.

269.
And if everyone's not joyful,
    It's because I'm feeling awful.
But life is so hard to predict:
    Always expect the unexpected!
My suitor plucks up the courage
    And asks for my hand in marriage.
Though it is sincerely meant,
    This is just not the right moment.

270.
He has built his hopes up too high,
    Imagining that somehow I'm free.
Sure the judgment has not been seen,
    It's being kept under lock and key.
His are flattering attentions,
    But this is no time for romance.
"Please see things from my point of view,
    This is about me, and not you.

I gave Oleśnicki my answer.

271.
I just can't give thought to it now.
    So I'm afraid, I must say no.
If I were you, I'd save your words
    For one of your other sweethearts.
It's always good to hedge your bets."
    He humbly accepts my regrets,
Struggling for some semblance of pride.
    He'll ask again. I'm sure of it.

He departed, having no hope.

272.
Freedom, when it comes, is so quiet.
    It's like nothing ever happened.
The old man's decided to up sticks,
    Having decamped and called it quits.
He has travelled all the way home,
    Having not taken Aesop with him.
As for my great protector: well,
    He's best removed from this scandal.

His Majesty the King also departed.

273.

Others enjoy the pleasantries
        Of Court, where there is gaiety
And flattery in abundance.
        But it's no place for damaged goods.
And how the Court loves to gossip
        About the fallen wife of Aesop!
"There's that fine convent in Lublin.
        So shouldn't she just become a nun?"

They advised me to live in a convent in Lublin.

Title:

Transakcyja… żałosne treny.

Translated here as "a transaction," *transakcyja* could also be rendered as "an account" of the course of a military campaign or war. A word rarely used in Polish, it was most notably elsewhere employed by Wacław Potocki for the title of his poetic chronicle *Transakcyja wojny chocimskiej* (A Transaction of the Chocim War, 1671). Stanisławska's world was so filled with death and lamentation, that the notion of mourning the tragedies of her own life, which left her with a sense of having no life left to her, seems an appropriate circumvention of the tradition of funerary lamentation.

To the Reader

The very title of the opening poem suggests that the entire work was intended for publication, and directed to a readership that was wider than her family and social circle. Not only does Stanisławska here justify lamenting a life still lived, but challenges men to overcome their prejudice and read a work that has been written by a woman.

"And having seen Fortune … lives robbed of happiness."

Stanisławska would agree with Ovid, who maintained that Fortune is unjust and wayward in her dealings with man. See Ovid, *Consolation to Livia*, 54.

"Let your good self press on … "

Stanisławska expects that men will take a scornful attitude to her work before reading so much as a page, even if, as she claims here, the calamitous dealings of Fortune are a universal affliction.

A Preamble of Dolor

Threnody I (Stanzas 1–8)

This threnody has many dream-like or visionary qualities. Here Stanisławska looks to escape from life at court and place herself in a naturalistic setting where she can be alone with her grief and recall the events of her life in quiet and contemplative surrounds. However, even in nature she is ill at ease and struggles with the fact that reflection can offer neither relief nor solace.

St. 2. "I shall not wade to the far side / of the Danube … water nymphs."

The Danube refers to the Battle of Vienna (1683), during which Stanisławska's third husband, Jan Zbąski, was mortally wounded. The stanza has also echoes of

Psalm 137.1, where the Jewish people, exiled in Babylon, sing of their yearning "by the waters" for their homeland, a yearning which gives way to vengeful exhortations against the children of Babylon.

St. 6–8. "Which fine leafy trees ... can hardly resist."
Here the poet in a margin note refers to the Stanisławski family's Pilawa coat of arms, which features the one-third cross (it is mentioned specifically in the poem's margin note to stanza 9). And whilst the tree denotes a wistful return to an idealized time before fate inflicted so many ordeals upon her, its symbolism merges the Tree of Wisdom, whose plucking by Eve precipitated The Fall, with that of The Cross, which symbolizes the great sacrifices of Stanisławska's generation.

The Pilawa Coat of Arms

The Hurts of Childhood
Threnody II (Stanzas 9–14)
Following the death of Stanisławska's aunt, Dominika Zebrzydowska, the prioress of the convent in Gródek outside Kraków, her grandfather Michał Zebrzydowski, the Voivode of Kraków in the years 1661–1667, became her guardian. However, Stanisławska remained in the convent, and whether she was free to explore the world beyond its walls during these years is unknown.

St. 12. "... jealous fate begrudged me this."
Here Stanisławska alludes principally to the loss she felt at the death of her aunt.

Vexation at the Fates
Threnody III (Stanzas 15–22)
Stanisławska reveals that her brother, Piotr, died at an early age, and she ascribes his death to the machinations of Fortune. Fortune, Stanisławska states, shares culpability with the traditions of the time, which insist that young people should be married at a young age. Instead of being a cause for celebration, for Stanisławska, this arranged marriage is nothing more than an occasion for regret and misery.

St. 19–20. "... deceive/ Me the way Laban did Jacob ... that if we could."
Prior to these stanzas, Stanisławska rejoices at having returned to her family home. Freedom, in hindsight, is what she would have wished for at this time. But if it came to a marital arrangement, she would have held out for a match that brought her happiness. The story of Jacob's marriage to Rachel and Leah does not align with Stanisławska's experience, but clearly she discerned a number of parallels. Recounted in Genesis 29, Jacob promises his shepherd uncle, Laban, seven years of service in return for Rachel, his youngest daughter. But on the wedding night, Laban delivers to Jacob his eldest, but weak-eyed daughter, Leah. Jacob and Leah make love, thus cementing their marriage. With the coming of morning, Jacob realizes what has transpired and reproaches Laban for his trickery. But to this Laban replies that it is custom to give the older daughter in marriage before the younger one. In order to appease Jacob, Laban offers him his younger daughter also in exchange for another seven years work. And so at the end of the week, Jacob ends up taking both sisters as his wives. Unsurprisingly, Jacob neglects Leah in favor of Rachel, but God takes pity on Leah and allows her to conceive four sons, making her a matriarch of Israel, whilst Rachel would remain childless. Stanisławska identifies principally with Jacob as the victim of Laban's deception. Just as Jacob had hoped to marry a woman of beauty and was thwarted in this, Stanisławska's expectations and dreams have been commensurately dashed.

St. 21–22. "Was he born amongst the tigers?... house-trained doe."
The Aesop of this poem is often mentioned in the same breath as the animals which featured in Aesop's fables. The intention here, however, is not to flatter, and the term "Lampart," meaning panther, is repeated in the margin note which states that "Lampart is a pig, who pleasured himself" [*Lampart jest świnią, co się sobą delektował*]. The question as to whether Aesop was "born amongst the tigers" must surely be rhetorical, and with a derisory edge to it. From what we are told, there was no question of Aesop ever having had the ability to "ravage" his wife. See Stanisław Szczęsny, "Anny ze Stanisławskich Zbąskiej opowieść o sobie i mężach: Glosa do barokowej trenodii," in Stasiewicz, *Pisarki polskie epok dawnych*, 81.

I Am to Marry into a House of Deviants
Threnodies IV–V (Stanzas 23–34)
With only two stanzas, Threnody IV sees Stanisławska blaming Fortune for poisoning her father's heart against her. Once the agreement has been made, her father and stepmother berate Stanisławska at every turn in order to ensure that she will be an amenable bride. The scolding continues in Threnody V. Even when Stanisławska's health suffers from the emotional distress, her parents only seem to want to make her well enough so that the marriage can take place.

St. 34. "We are busy about the town ... "

Stanisławska and her parents were present in Warsaw on March 1, 1668, when they and other magnate families accompanied Sobieski, who, on the back of a number of military victories to the East, entered Warsaw to great pomp and fanfare. See Tadeusz Korzon, *Dola i niedola Jana Sobieskiego, 1629–1674*, vol. 2 (Kraków: Wydawnictwo Akademii Umiejętności, 1898), 68.

The Wedding

Threnody VI (Stanzas 35–43)

We are presented with our first depiction of Aesop, who seems to have no idea as to the purpose of his journey. It is a comical episode, but Stanisławska's terror and disgust at the sight of her betrothed is alluded to in vivid detail. Again, she emphasizes the part played by her parents in forcing her to participate in the wedding ceremony, and as she takes her vows, the threats of her stepmother are literally ringing in her ears.

St. 39. "The Bishop ... "

Presumably this bishop was the Bishop of Kraków, and his presence would be understandable given that it was the son of the Castellan of Kraków who was getting married.

The Wedding Banquet and Later

Threnody VII–VIII (Stanzas 44–56)

Stanisławska's scathing assessment of the oratorical abilities of the Voivode of Lublin, Władysław Rej (1612–1682), illustrates her formidable intolerance of pomposity and cant.

St. 46. "... the great voivode ... tortured wretch."

A direct descendant of the Father of Polish literature, Mikołaj Rej (1505–1569), Władysław Rej enjoyed a reputation for conviviality and great oratorical skills. However, in the poem Stanisławska does her best to make little of Rej's reputation in this regard. Like the Warszyckis, a year later, Rej would support the successful candidature of Michał Korybut Wiśniowiecki for the Polish-Lithuanian crown. One can imagine that this wedding represented an opportunity for senators and noblemen to discuss the floundering reign of Jan II Kazimierz Waza, who would abdicate later that year, in September 1668.

St. 51. "... dancing in his delia."

A winter over-garment of the Polish nobility, which accorded with the oriental tastes of the time. Several portraits of personages such as Jan Zamojski and Jan Sobieski depict them posing in delia coats, which show a richly colored robe that has short, loose sleeves, and metal buttons which clasp the cloak at the breast. The collar was generally finished with fur.

The Old Man's Terms
Threnody IX (Stanzas 57–76)
The festivities continue for several days, and for all this time the union remains unconsummated. Meanwhile, Stanisławska's parents give thought to the domestic arrangements of the young couple and they delicately broach the topic with the Castellan. Firstly, Stanisławska's stepmother tries to get assurances that the young couple will be allowed to live independently on their own estate. But she soon realizes that the Castellan has no intention of allowing this, and takes the news to her husband, who is both appalled and furious in equal measure. There follows a comedic shoot-the-messenger episode, where the one-eyed priest shuttles between the two magnates and delivers demand and counter-demand. Stanisławska's father, now aggrieved at the idea of his daughter being married to a man who is incapable of running his own household, is only mollified when the Castellan gives assurances that his supervision will be a transitional arrangement. The priest's role here must surely have succeeded not only in keeping the men apart but also in preventing an escalation of the dispute, which could have had wider political consequences.

St. 74. "That men hold your word in great store."
However, according to Lublin law records, the Castellan failed to pay a debt to Jan Nehrebski in the sum of 1,200 zlotys, and thus risked having the title of infamy associated with his name. He eventually undertook to pay the debt and offered Nehrebski a diamond ring as a sign of good faith. Nehrebski returned the ring with the expectation that the debt would be paid. Having so tricked his creditor into essentially forgiving the debt, the Castellan never repaid the outstanding sum. See Kotowa, *Transakcyja*, 214, note to stanza 74.

The First Days of My Bondage
Threnody X (Stanzas 77–88)
This threnody recounts the final day of the wedding festivities, by which time the guests and Stanisławska's family have had plenty of time to observe and form an opinion about Aesop's behavior. Stanisławska's vulnerable situation could not have been lost on anyone. Aesop still does not seem to register the fact that he is now married. Attendant women nudge and prod Aesop, but their efforts prove futile. The threnody ends with the departure of the Castellan, having settled that Stanisławska and Aesop will follow a number of days later. Stanisławska's father attempts to get to know his son-in-law better but realizes—if he had not done so before—that he is dealing with someone who is irredeemably unbalanced. Aesop

shows that he is bereft of any masculine traits, exemplified by his inability to ride a horse. When Aesop is thrown from his horse in a hunt, such is the perceived shame that the hunting party decide not to tell Stanisławska about the incident.

My Father's Great Remorse
Threnody XI (Stanzas 89–92)
Michał now knows that he has placed his daughter in great danger and bitterly reproaches himself for his actions. He considers aloud how he may prevent his daughter from undertaking the journey to the Castellan's home, and to the great unknown that awaits her. He gives serious consideration to keeping Stanisławska at home but is then advised against acting so impulsively.

St. 89. "And set off to war once again."
In May 1668, fearing an attack from Ottoman forces, Sobieski summoned the nobility to defend the Commonwealth's borders to the southeast, near Lwów.

Saying Farewell to My Beloved Father
Threnody XII (Stanzas 93–100)
With the beginning of this threnody, Stanisławska and Aesop have arrived at the Castellan's home and a meagre feast is laid on for the guests. Aesop, on his own home turf, behaves as waywardly and erratically as ever, and there can be little in his comportment that offers comfort to either Michał or Stanisławska. As her father departs, Stanisławska accompanies him for a short distance and is then bidden to return. It is a heartrending episode, and we can only imagine how lonely and fearful Stanisławska was at this time.

St. 93. "We're all sitting down to the feast ... "
This feast may have taken place in the Castellan's stronghold of Danków Castle, which is to be found in north Silesia. Here is where Stanisławska presumably resided for the first months of her marriage.

St. 97. "He is stupid. She is too young."
Jan Bieniecki, a friend of the Stanisławski family. Stanisławska held his son Franciszek in more affection, as can be seen in the letter addressed to him towards the end of her life, which is the only correspondence by Stanisławska to have remained extant.

St. 99. "Tries to give me consolation ... of affection."
If it is not entirely clear in the poem proper, the margin note states clearly that the Castellan propositioned his daughter-in-law.

My Hateful Life with Aesop
Threnody XIII (Stanzas 101–19)
This threnody begins with a dispute between Bieniecki and the Castellan, who wants his own man to run the household in his absence. Not for the first time does the Castellan's scheming raise the ire of Stanisławska's father, but the quarrel is soon resolved. Though exceedingly amusing in its telling, the account of Stanisławska's life with Aesop is a litany of outrageous acts wherein Aesop subjects his wife to repeated psychological and physical abuse. But Stanisławska is not the only victim, as Aesop is also shown to be a tyrant towards his subjects.

My Father Dies
Threnody XIV (Stanzas 120–25)
In an encampment outside Lwów, where the forces of other Commonwealth magnates are gathered, Stanisławska's father falls ill with dysentery. He asks to be brought to a trusted friend in Stratyn near Lwów. However, his retinue takes the wrong road and brings him to the village of Podkamień, the site of a Dominican monastic complex. Here the previous two husbands of his present wife had also died, and so Michał takes their accidental presence in Podkamień as a portent of his imminent death. In his last will and testament Michał assigns his daughter powerful guardians, including Jan Sobieski, Hetman of the Commonwealth. Michał Stanisławski died in early February, 1668, and was buried in Lwów on February 18. See Korzon, *Dola i niedola*, 168.

St. 121. "… to the home of his niece."
Anna Silnicka, the wife of Gabriel Silnicki, who was one of the great military Polish commanders of his era. Silnicki was also named by Michał Stanisławski as a guardian of his daughter. See Kotowa, *Transakcyja*, 215, note to stanza 121.

St. 122. "The voivode could do little more."
Here the poet is referring to the Voivode of Rus, Stanisław Jan Jabłonowski (1663–1772), who loyally served Sobieski in countless campaigns. Like Sobieski, he would support the French candidate, Louis de Bourbon, Prince of Condé, in the Polish royal election of June 1669. For an autobiographical account, see Marek Wagner, *Stanisław Jabłonowski, 1634–1702: Kasztelan krakowski i hetman wielki koronny* (Warsaw: Mada, 2000).

St. 125. "Behold the fire-eyed maid, Bellona!"
Bellona was a Roman goddess of war and was often depicted with a helmet, spear and torch. For Wacław Potocki, the war-ridden age in which they lived was one governed by the personification of cruel Bellona. See Krystyna Złotkowska, "Ślady

krwawej Bellony w twórczości Wacława Potockiego," *Słupskie prace filologiczne: Seria filologia polska* 4 (2005): 55–78.

They Conspire to Conceal My Father's Death from Me
Threnody XV (Stanzas 126–40)
The decision by the Castellan to withhold from Stanisławska the news of her father's death is rather puzzling, as surely her position was weaker than it had ever been. Perhaps time was needed to see what the legal position was pertaining to Stanisławska's inheritance. He would also have given consideration to the issue of Stanisławska's appointed guardians, intuiting perhaps that they may wish to deliver Stanisławska from her predicament. Observing the behavior of the household, Stanisławska senses that something is amiss. Eventually Aesop, in defiance of his father's wishes, blurts out the terrible truth.

St. 128. "The old man calls us to Lublin."
Stanisławska was owed a sum of money from Marianna Zebrzydowska arising from the death of her husband the Voivode of Kraków, Michał Zebrzydowski. Mention of the case is to be found in Lublin's law records. See Kotowa, *Transakcyja*, 215–216, note to stanza 128.

St. 130. "We spend the night … home of Firlej."
Stanisław Warszycki's daughter, Teresa, was married to the Castellan of Lublin, Jan Firlej, whose family estate and castle were to be found in the small village of Markuszów, situated in the voivodeship of Lublin.

St. 135. "But you'll find your aunt … at death's door."
Stanisławska's aunt on her mother's side was Anna Lanckorońska. However, the aunt in question here seems to be her father's sister, Konstancja Stanisławska, who was first married to Krzysztof Koniecpolski (with whom she had one son, Jan Koniecpolski), and who was married at the time of this account to Kazimierz Grudziński. The available genealogical records are unclear as to both her birth and death, but 1669 is given as the possible year of her demise, a date which would give some credence to this account.

I Come to Know the Devastating Truth
Threnody XV–XVI (Stanzas 141–54)
Aesop is jubilant at the sight of his heart-broken and traumatized wife, but when the Castellan hears of his betrayal, he thrashes Aesop with a stick. Both the Castellan and his wife try to comfort Stanisławska, but she will not accept such kindnesses. Here Stanisławska must also litigate with her stepmother for the rights to her father's estate of Maciejowice. Stanisławska wins this case, which

allows her to return home. Now that she is out from under the controlling eye of the Castellan, she can set about extricating herself from the marriage.

St. 150. "My stepmother hatches plans, / Stashing away my belongings."
As revealed by Stanisławska's letter to Franciszek Bieniecki, dated May 23, 1699, Stanisławska's stepmother had been willed much of her husband's property, which was to remain in her possession for the rest of her life.

I Try to Take Aesop in Hand
Threnody XVII (Stanzas 155–65)

Even though Aesop's behavior is as outlandish as ever, Stanisławska is now more capable of handling her appendage. She even tries to persuade Aesop to request of the Hetmans that her father's martial banner be conferred upon him. Martial endeavor was regarded by the Polish nobility as character-forming and crucial to a young man's education. See Aleksandra Skrzypietz, *Królewscy synowie: Jakub, Aleksander i Konstanty Sobiescy* (Katowice: Wydawnictwo Uniwersytetu Śląskiego, 2011), 51–52. But Aesop suspects, and not without justification, that this would be tantamount to volunteering to lead men in the many military campaigns that his peers and contemporaries were bravely undertaking.

St. 158. "… the Hetmans."
Hetmans were the main commanders of the Polish forces and were only second to the king in the chain of command. There were two Grand Hetmans, one for the Polish and one for the Lithuanian armies, and each had an assistant called a Field Hetman, who would command the army in their absence.

I Am Too Ill to Travel to My Father's Funeral
Threnody XVIII (Stanzas 166–71)

Stanisławska undertakes the journey to Lwów where her father's funeral is due to take place. However, she falls ill and must return home to convalesce. The final stanza reveals a bedridden Stanisławska performing her own funerary rite and commending her father's soul into God's care.

The First Chink of Light
Threnody XIX (Stanzas 172–79)

Word is brought to Stanisławska that her family and guardians are making plans to rescue her. They must proceed with care lest an accident befall her: as has been seen, the poisoning of troublesome wives was not uncommon. But the Castellan gets wind that something is afoot and sends his one-eyed priest to speak to Stanisławska so as to discern her state of mind. Stanisławska proves to be more than a match for the priest and sends him away convinced that she has found contentment in marriage. This episode could happily belong in Book Seven of Boccaccio's *The Decameron*, where the female heroines display their superior craftiness and cunning, albeit mostly at the expense of their husbands. Although Boccaccio's *The Decameron* was not published in Poland until the late nineteenth century, threads of his stories had reached Poland by the sixteenth century because of the close cultural and diplomatic ties between Poland and the Italian states. See Krzysztof Żaboklicki, *Giovanni Boccaccio* (Warsaw: Wiedza Powszechna, 1980), 367–88.

St. 174. "The priest ... master of his art."

The episode echoes in spirit the story told in *The Decameron* 7:5, wherein a jealous husband disguises himself as a priest and hears his wife's confession. She tells him that she loves a priest, and in response to this he keeps a vigil at her door every evening in the hope of intercepting his rival. However, his wife had known of her husband's ploy all along, and whilst he guarded the door she was able to let her lover into the room through the window.

My Family Comes to My Aid

Threnody XX (Stanzas 180–85)

This is a very intriguing episode. Stanisławska meets her guardian and protector, Jan Sobieski, who immediately advises her to resolve all differences with her stepmother. Sobieski asks Stanisławska to be magnanimous and forgive her stepmother's complicity in having married her off to a deviant. We may only surmise that Sobieski arranged this meeting with the permission of the Castellan, who must have felt that to refuse the Hetman a meeting with his charge would have been regarded as an intolerable insult.

St. 183. "When the throne is vacated ... life as an abbot."

Jan II Kazimierz Waza abdicated the Polish-Lithuanian throne on September 16, 1668. He returned to France and joined the Jesuit order. His lineage must have greatly shortened his novitiate, however, as he was soon made Abbot of the Benedictine Abbey of Saint-Germain-des-Prés, a position he held until his death in 1672.

I Enter the Sanctuary of the Convent

Threnody XXI–XXII (Stanzas 186–202)

Preoccupied with the royal election, the Castellan thought he had acted prudently by placing Stanisławska in a convent, but it must have dawned on him almost immediately that he had made a great error of judgment. Aesop was perhaps even more intuitive and had a sense of what was afoot. He made desperate attempts to drag his wife out of the convent but could only resort to making violent, ugly scenes. But Stanisławska was now safely ensconced in an inviolate place. Worn out and weary from nervous exhaustion, Stanisławska falls ill, which serves to satisfy an increasingly alarmed Castellan that the reason for Stanisławska's extended stay in the convent can be put down to her poor health. Of course, because of the election, the city of Warsaw is thronging with the good and the great and their families, and soon people are talking about this unfolding drama.

St. 191. "Aesop's brother-in-law."

Future Sword-Bearer of the Crown and a hero of the Battle of Vienna, Michał Warszycki was the son of the Castellan's brother, Aleksander. With a dispensation from Rome, Michał married the Castellan's daughter, Anna.

St. 196. "... she who wears a miter."

Katarzyna Radziwiłłowa, the sister of Jan Sobieski, and the wife of magnate Michał Kazimierz Radziwiłł (1625–1680). Katarzyna would have empathized with Stanisławska's plight more than most, as in her youth she had been forced to marry the unsightly and much older Duke Władysław Dominik Zasławski-Ostrogski. However, she had given her heart to Michał Kazimierz Radziwiłł and embarked on an affair with him only two weeks after her wedding day. Fortunately for Katarzyna, her husband was a tolerant sort and chose to turn a blind eye to his wife's shenanigans. Władysław had the good grace to die not long after the nuptials, which meant that Katarzyna was then free to marry the man she loved. See Maria Bogucka, *Women in Early Polish Society, against the European Background* (Aldershot, UK: Ashgate, 2004), 6–7.

I Make Peace with My Stepmother

Threnody XXIII (Stanzas 203–16)

Here Stanisławska concedes much of her property to her stepmother in negotiations overseen by advisors appointed by the Castellan. However, these same advisors do not know that the two women are in league with one another. Presumably the ruse here involves wresting back ownership of some of Stanisławska's estate from the Castellan so that her stepmother may make restitution to Stanisławska following the annulment. One way or another, Stanisławska is taking a leap of faith. And as events transpire, her stepmother will prove to be her staunchest and most crucial ally in the annulment proceedings. In the meantime, the Castellan is set on bringing Stanisławska back home by fair means or foul. When his plot to kidnap Stanisławska is foiled, he sends Aesop to demand of his wife that she return to the marital fold. But Aesop's shambolic efforts at charm and persuasion are given short shrift from Stanisławska and Sobieski. The threnody closes with a secret gathering of Stanisławska and her guardians.

St. 211. "But I am forewarned … cares a jot."
The person alluded to here is once again Michał Warszycki, Aesop's brother-in-law. Michał may have been acting in good faith but it seems that the poet had no wish to express gratitude to any member of the Warszycki family.

St. 216. "One lady … "
Numbered amongst the conspiratorial gathering is Helena Lubomirska, the wife of Aleksander Lubomirski, the recently appointed Voivode of Kraków.

I Declare My Intentions
Threnody XXIV (Stanzas 217–23)
This is a triumphant moment where Stanisławska shows that she has the measure of not only her guardians, whom she feels would be happy to leave her in the convent, but also the Castellan himself. She is not afraid to say firstly to her guardians, and then at a later time to the Castellan, that she wishes to be rid of Aesop forever, and that she will proceed fearlessly until she obtains an annulment. It is somewhat telling that Stanisławska has the last word in this threnody, and that she does not reveal the Castellan's response. Perhaps he had been rendered speechless.

Aesop Begs Me to Reconsider
Threnody XXV (Stanzas 224–28)
This final meeting with Aesop shows that Stanisławska had begun to take the upper hand in the marriage and that perhaps she could have exercised in the long run some positive influence over her husband. Aesop is certainly contrite here. He knows that a divorce will result in him being left once again at the mercy of his father's tyranny.

St. 224. "To the Papal Nuncio … "
The Papal Nuncio to Poland at the time was Galeazzo Mariscotti, who held the office from March 1668 to August 1670.

St. 227. "Don't leave me, my sweet Anusiu! … my Kazusiu!"
The translation here keeps the diminutive appellatives of the names "Anna" and "Kazimierz." In this instance, such appellatives would generally denote a loving marital relationship.

The Old Man Corrupts Proceedings and I Have Suitors
Threnody XXVI (Stanzas 229–40)
The Castellan proves to be a wily and formidable opponent. Not only does he manage to bribe the judge, but he also threatens the nuns of the convent where

Stanisławska is residing with the withdrawal of his benefaction. However, Sobieski keeps the hearing on track and puts the judge in his place. The Papal Nuncio also gets involved and makes sure that the nuns continue to offer Stanisławska sanctuary without fear or favor. Amazingly, whilst still within the walls of the convent, Stanisławska begins to receive proposals of marriage, but she remains unimpressed by all the flattery and attention. The fact that she had suitors whilst still married must also point to the fact that bachelors and maidens of the Polish nobility had a very small pool of potential spouses to choose from.

St. 235. "Looking to the one he trusts most … "

Here the person in question was Stanisławska's first cousin, Jan Stanisław Koniecpolski, the son of her paternal aunt, Konstancja Stanisławska and Krzysztof Koniecpolski. As we read in the Introduction, in spite of the great service which he renders Stanisławska during this time, in later years Koniecpolski, as Stanisławska's sole heir, will take action to secure his inheritance and look to prevent his cousin from divesting any more of her property to the Church.

The Court Finds in My Favor but Calls for an Inquisition

Threnody XXVII (Stanzas 241–47)

The court grants the annulment on condition that witnesses can be produced who will verify that Stanisławska was indeed forced up the aisle by her father. Stanisławska is able to produce witnesses who can confirm her version of events. However, the evidence given by Stanisławska's stepmother imputes both her own honor and that of her recently departed husband. Her testimony leaves no doubt in anyone's mind that this was a forced marriage, and was therefore distinguishable in law from the spirit of an arranged marriage.

St. 242 "The judgment stipulates… twelve witnesses."

It seems that although the judge found in favor of Stanisławska on the principle that a forced marriage is unjust, it was then beholden on the plaintiff to provide witnesses who could establish for the record the true course of events. The defendants also had the right to produce witnesses, but their testimony must have been exposed with ease as a tissue of lies.

I Am Granted a Divorce but I Must Return Everything

Threnody XXVIII (Stanzas 248–65)

The judge has the last word, and even though he finds in favor of Stanisławska, his judgment comes with a terrible stipulation, which states that all wedding gifts must be returned to Aesop, his family and guests. The Warszyckis, making the most of this opportunity to exact a modicum of vengeance, insist that Stanisławska return every last trinket and garment.

St. 254. "He would have beaten… not intervened."
The fact that the king elect sent an envoy to mediate between Stanisławska and the Warszyckis concerning the matter of the necklace, illustrates the extent to which the divorce had drawn in so many illustrious figures of the era.

A New Proposal of Marriage and Bittersweet Freedom
Threnody XXIX (Stanzas 266–73)

Stanisławska fulfils her obligations in respect of the judgment and is now free. However, the Warszyckis make one more appeal to Rome, which means that Stanisławska has to remain in the convent. When this appeal is rejected, the Warszyckis lift their siege of the convent and return home. By rights, Stanisławska should be ecstatic at this favorable turn of events, but she is emotionally exhausted, and feels, perhaps unjustifiably, that her supporters have slunk away so as to distance themselves from the whiff of scandal which now surrounds her. However, almost as if she were a widow, Stanisławska has now the freedom to choose a husband, but she chooses to spurn the advances of a handsome and dashing suitor, Jan Oleśnicki, who has declared his ardor.

St. 268. "… the coronation."
The coronation of Michał Korybut Wiśniowiecki took place in Kraków on September 29, 1669.

St. 272. "As for my great protector … scandal."
After the coronation, Sobieski retreated to his estate in the Ukraine, where he soon had to devote all his attentions to protecting the southeastern border of the Commonwealth from Tatar and Cossack incursions. Sobieski's wife, Marysieńka, did make friendly overtures to the new king, however, and attended his wedding to Eleanor Maria Josefa of Austria, which took place in the monastery of Jasna Góra in February of 1670. With her husband encamped in Firlejówka near Lwów, the pregnant Marysieńka undertook a journey to Paris at the end of May. However, she went into labor somewhere between Brussels and Paris, and gave birth prematurely to a baby daughter, who died soon after. See Korzon, *Dola i niedola*, 440.

Bibliography

Published Works of Anna Stanisławska

Transakcyja albo opisanie całego życia jednej sieroty przez żałosne treny od tejże samej pisane roku 1685 (A Transaction, or an Account of the Entire Life of an Orphan Girl by way of Plaintful Threnodies in the Year 1685). Edited by Ida Kotowa, with Introduction and critical notes. Kraków: Polska Akademia Umiejętności, 1935.

Transakcyja albo opisanie całego życia jednej sieroty przez żałosne treny od tejże samej pisane roku 1685: Fragmenty (A Transaction, or an Account of the Entire Life of an Orphan Girl by way of Plaintful Threnodies in the Year 1685: Fragments). Edited by Piotr Borek. Kraków: Universitas, 2003.

Secondary Sources

Abramowska, Janina. *Polska bajka ezopowa* (Poland's Aesop Fable). Poznań: Wydawnictwo Naukowe UAM, 1991.

Bieńkowski, Tadeusz. "Panegiryk a życie literackie w Polsce XVI i XVII wieku" (Panegyric and Literary Life in 16th- and 17th-Century Poland). In *Z dziejów życia literackiego w Polsce XVI i XVII wieku (A History of Literary Life in 16th- and 17th-Century Poland)*, edited by Hanna Dziechcińska, 183–96. Wrocław: Zakład Narodowy im. Ossolińskich, 1980.

Bogucka, Maria. *The Lost World of the "Sarmatians": Custom as the Regulator of Polish Social Life in Early Modern Times.* Warsaw: Polish Academy of Sciences, Institute of History, 1996.

__________. *Women in Early Polish Society, against the European Background.* Aldershot, UK: Ashgate, 2004.

Brückner, Aleksander. *Dzieje kultury polskiej: Polska u szczytu potęgi* (A History of Polish Culture: Poland at the Peak of its Power), vol. 2. 2nd ed. Warsaw: Książka i Wiedza, 1958.

__________. *Dzieje literatury polskiej w zarysie* (A Concise History of Polish Culture), vol. 1. Warsaw: Gebethner i Wolff, 1908.

__________. "Wiersze zbieranej drużyny: Pierwsza autorka polska i jej autobiografia wierszem" (Gathered Poems: The First Polish Woman Author and her Autobiography in Verse). *Biblioteka Warszawska* 4 (1893): 424–29.

Bystroń, Jan Stanisław. *Dzieje obyczajów w dawnej Polsce: wiek XVI–XVIII* (Customs and Traditions in Old Poland: 16th–18th century), vol. 1. 2nd ed. Warsaw: Państwowy Instytut Wydawniczy, 1976.

Davies, Norman. *God's Playground: A History of Poland, vol. 1: The Origins to 1795*. Oxford: Clarendon Press, 1981.

Dziechcińska, Hanna. *Ciało, strój, gest w czasach renesansu i baroku* (Body, Dress and Gesture in the Renaissance and Baroque Times). Warsaw: Państwowe Wydawnictwo Naukowe, 1981.

__________. *Kultura literacka w Polsce XVI i XVII wieku: Zagadnienia wybrane* (Literary Culture in 16th- and 17th-Century Poland: Selected Issues). Warsaw: Wydawnictwo Naukowe Semper, 1994.

__________. *Literatura a zabawa: Z dziejów kultury literackiej w dawnej Polsce* (Literature and Play: A History of the Literary Culture of Old Poland). Warsaw: Państwowe Wydawnictwo Naukowe, 1981.

Fei, Alfred. "Z poezji staropolskiej: Jan Smolik – Anna Stanisławska" (From the Poetry of Old Poland: Jan Smolik – Anna Stanisławska). *Pamiętnik Literacki* 1–4 (1936): 815–40.

Frost, Robert I. *After the Deluge: Poland-Lithuania and the Second Northern War, 1655–1660*. Cambridge: Cambridge University Press, 2003.

Hopp, Lajos. "Sobieski a orientacja profrancuska malkontentów węgierskich" (Sobieski and the Pro-French Orientation of the Hungarian Malcontents). In *Studia z dziejów epoki Jana III Sobieskiego* (Studies on the Era of Jan III Sobieski), edited by Krystyn Matwijowski et al., 47–62. Wrocław: Wydawnictwo Uniwersytetu Wrocławskiego, 1984.

Jasienica, Paweł. *Polska anarchia* (The Polish Anarchy). Kraków: Wydawnictwo Literackie, 1988.

Korzon, Tadeusz. *Dola i niedola Jana Sobieskiego, 1629–1674* (The Fortunes and Misfortunes of Jan Sobieski, 1629–1674), vol. 2. Kraków: Wydawnictwo Akademii Umiejętności, 1898.

Kotowa, Ida. "Anna Stanisławska: Pierwsza autorka polska" (Anna Stanisławska: The First Polish Woman Author). *Pamiętnik Literacki* 1–4 (1934): 267–90.

Kuchowicz, Zbigniew. *Obyczaje staropolskie XVII–XVIII wieku* (Old Polish Traditions and Customs in the 17th and 18th Centuries). Łódź: Wydawnictwo Łódzkie, 1974.

Mikulski, Tadeusz. "Drobiazgi staropolskie: Anna Zbąska ze Stanisławskich" (Trinkets of Old Poland: Anna Zbąska of the Stanisławski Line). *Ruch Literacki* 7–8 (1935): 202–3.

Miłosz, Czesław. *The History of Polish Literature*. Berkeley: University of California Press, 1983.

Peretz, Maya. "In Search of the First Polish Woman Author." *The Polish Review* 38, no. 4 (1993): 469–83.

Phillips, Ursula. "Piszące białogłowy od średniowiecza do końca XVIII wieku" (Women Writers from the Middle Ages to the End of the 18th Century). In *Pisarki polskie od średniowiecza do współczesności: przewodnik* (Polish

Women Writers from the Middle Ages to Contemporary Times: a Guide), edited by Grażyna Borkowska, Małgorzata Czermińska, and Ursula Phillips, 5–16. Gdańsk: Wydawnictwo Słowo/Obraz Terytoria, 2000.

Podhorecki, Leszek. *Jan Karol Chodkiewicz, 1560–1621*. Warsaw: Wydawnictwo Ministerstwa Obrony Narodowej, 1982.

Popławska, Halina. "'Żałosne treny' Anny Stanisławskiej" ('The Doleful Laments' of Anna Stanisławska). In *Pisarki polskie epok dawnych* (Polish Women Writers of Olden Times), edited by Krystyna Stasiewicz, 89–111. Olsztyn: Wyższa Szkoła Pedagogiczna, 1998.

Rott, Dariusz. *Kobieta z przemalowanego portretu* (The Woman from the Retouched Portrait). Katowice: Wydawnictwo Uniwersytetu Śląskiego, 2004.

Sajkowski, Alojzy. *Staropolska miłość: Z dawnych listów i pamiętników* (Love in Old Poland: From Letters and Diaries). Poznań: Wydawnictwo Poznańskie, 1981.

Sinko, Tadeusz. "Trzy małżeństwa jednej sieroty" (The Three Marriages of an Orphan Girl). *Czas* 109 (1935): 5.

Skrzypietz, Aleksandra. *Królewscy synowie: Jakub, Aleksander i Konstanty Sobiescy* (Royal Sons: Jakub, Aleksander and Konstanty Sobieski). Katowice: Wydawnictwo Uniwersytetu Śląskiego, 2011.

Sokolski, Jacek. *Bogini, pojęcie, demon: Fortuna w dziełach autorów staropolskich* (Goddess, Idea, Demon: Fortune in the Works of the Authors of Old Poland). Wrocław: Wydawnictwo Uniwersytetu Wrocławskiego, 1996.

Stieber, Zdzisław. "Przyczynki do historii polskich rymów, 1. Rymy sandomierskie XVI i XVII wieku" (Contributions to the History of Polish Rhymes, 1. Sandomierz Rhymes of the 16th and 17th Centuries). *Język Polski* 3 (1950): 110–13.

Stone, Daniel. *The Polish-Lithuanian State, 1386–1795*. Seattle: University of Washington Press, 2001.

Szczęsny, Stanisław. "Anny ze Stanisławskich Zbąskiej opowieść o sobie i mężach: Glosa do barokowej trenodii" (Anna Zbąska of the Stanisławski Family—A Tale about her Life and her Husbands: A Commentary to a Baroque Threnody). In *Pisarki polskie epok dawnych* (Polish Women Writers of Olden Times), edited by Krystyna Stasiewicz, 69–87. Olsztyn: Wyższa Szkoła Pedagogiczna, 1998.

Targosz, Karolina. *Sawantki w Polsce XVII wieku: Aspiracje intelektualne kobiet ze środowisk dworskich* (Savantes in 17th-Century Poland: The Intellectual Aspirations of Courtly Women). Warsaw: Retro-Art, 1997.

Tazbir, Janusz. *Studia nad kulturą staropolską* (A Study on the Culture of Old Poland). Kraków: TAiWPN Universitas, 2001.

Wagner, Marek. *Stanisław Jabłonowski, 1634–1702: Kasztelan krakowski i hetman wielki koronny* (Stanisław Jabłonowski, 1634–1702: Castellan of Kraków and Grand Crown Hetman). Warsaw: Mada, 2000.

Żaboklicki, Krzysztof. *Giovanni Boccaccio.* Warsaw: Wiedza Powszechna, 1980.
Złotkowska, Krystyna. "Ślady krwawej Bellony w twórczości Wacława Potockiego" (The Traces of Bloody Bellona in the Poetry of Wacław Potocki). *Słupskie prace filologiczne: Seria filologia polska* 4 (2005): 55–78.
Żółkiewski, Stanisław. *Początek i progres wojny moskiewskiej* (The Beginnings and Progress of the Muscovite War). Warsaw: Gebethner i Wolff, 1920.

Index